WARRIORS OF THE NORTH
UNION LEADERS OF THE CIVIL WAR

American History Archives™

Warriors of the North
Union Leaders of the Civil War

4 5 6 7 / 12 11 10 09
ISBN 978-1-58159-245-0

The History Channel Club
c/o North American Membership Group
12301 Whitewater Drive
Minnetonka, MN 55343
www.thehistorychannelclub.com

Published by North American Membership Group under license from Osprey
Publishing Ltd.

Previously published as Elite 73: *American Civil War Commanders (1) Union
Leaders in the East* and Elite 89: *American Civil War Commanders (3) Union
Leaders in the West* by Osprey Publishing, Midland House, West Way, Botley,
Oxford OX2 0PH, United Kingdom

© 2005 Osprey Publishing Ltd.   OSPREY
PUBLISHING

Editor: Martin Windrow
Design: Alan Hamp
Index by Glyn Sutcliffe
Originated by PPS Grasmere, Leeds, UK
Printed in China through World Print Ltd.

FRONT COVER
Ulysses S. Grant, ca. 1860–ca. 1865. (NARA)

Author's Note

Within this book the commanders covered have been divided
between the "Eastern" and "Western" theaters of war, according to
their first, most important, or best-known operations.

It should perhaps be emphasized that there is obviously no
space in this format for more than the most basic notes on the
careers of some of the giants of the war like Lee, Jackson, Grant
and Sherman. The author has tried to give a flavor of their
characters and appearance through the words of those who knew
them, but for any serious analysis of their command service the
reader is directed to the existing substantial biographies.

While American conventions of spelling and punctuation have
been used throughout this text, readers will notice historical
variations in passages directly quoted from writings of the period.

Acknowledgements

All monochrome illustrations in this book are from the collection of
Military Images magazine.

Artist's Note

**Author PHILIP KATCHER was born in Los Angeles, California,
to parents involved in the film industry. He was educated at
the University of Maryland and served in the
US Army in Vietnam. He has also been an active participant
in living history activities, especially in the 18th and
19th century periods. He has written a number of books
on various periods of US military history and presently is
editor/publisher of *Military Images Magazine*.**

**Illustrator RICHARD HOOK was born in 1938 and trained at
Reigate College of Art. After national service with 1st Bn,
Queen's Royal Regiment he became art editor of the much-
praised magazine *Finding Out* during the 1960s. He has
worked as a freelance illustrator ever since, earning an
international reputation particularly for his deep knowledge
of Native American material culture; and has illustrated more
than 30 Osprey titles. Richard is married and lives in Sussex.**

WARRIORS OF THE NORTH
Union Leaders of the Civil War

CONTENTS

INTRODUCTION

The men who led the Union Army to victory in the American Civil War were not a fancy or flamboyant lot. This is in stark contrast to their Confederate counterparts.

Although they may not have possessed all the tactical brilliance or dramatic style the Southern leaders enjoyed, the generals who finally led the North to victory shared one key trait among themselves: They were dogged and determined brawlers, unafraid of anything. They were warriors, pure and simple. And they led by brave example … directly into the teeth of battle.

As an example of Northern leadership style, the man who ultimately led the North to victory, Ulysses S. Grant, preferred to wear the uniform of a private over that of a general. Another key figure on the road to Northern victory employed a revolutionary new kind of battle plan, destroying a 60-mile-wide swath of the Confederacy on his March to the Sea; William T. Sherman brought the rebels to their knees.

Here are the stories of the brave and persistent soldiers who led the Union to ultimate victory.

In Part 1—Union Leaders in the East, you'll meet the men who led troops in the Eastern theater of war. In many cases, their proximity to reporters and the capital hindered their efforts; they were always under scrutiny, often to the point of paralysis.

In Part 2—Union Leaders in the West, you'll discover the generals who, literally, fought their way to the top. These are the men who ultimately brought victory home—no easy task against leaders and soldiers as magnificent as the Confederacy's. These men knew that a war further dragged out was a war lost. So they delivered the necessary knockout blows.

America's history—and in particular the details about the Civil War—is about much more than just dates and places. It's also about the people who made things happen. Here's a chance to discover essential details behind the *Warriors of the North—Union Leaders of the Civil War.*

OPPOSITE **The brash, self-confident Joseph Hooker, seen here while still a brigadier-general, would be appointed to command the Army of the Potomac in December 1862. He lost his nerve, and the battle, at Chancellorsville the following May. Sent West, he regained his reputation with the public but not with his fellow generals, who never trusted him – he had a reputation for insincerity and back-biting behind his affable manner.**

The mid-19th-century photographic process points up the contrast of the dark blue velvet collar and cuffs against the cloth of his coat; he wears a crimson line officer's sash. Note the hilt of the staff officer's sword, with a general officer's gold cord knot.

PART 1
UNION LEADERS IN THE EAST

INTRODUCTION

THE ORGANIZATION OF THE United States Army in 1861 was based on the needs of a nation basically at peace, with no borders to guard against an aggressive enemy, and a traditional national distrust of large standing armies. The army had no units larger than a regiment, and even these regiments rarely came together as a single force, being largely dispersed among many separate and often remote forts in company strength. As a result the army felt no need for any rank higher than a major-general, while brigadier-generals would command brigades assembled on an as-needed basis. The senior general, who had been Winfield Scott for as long as most Americans could remember, was designated the Major-General Commanding the Army, but he was the only man ever to hold this particular rank.

Generals usually came from the ranks of the graduates of the US Military Academy at West Point, New York (Winfield Scott, who had been appointed directly before the War of 1812, was an exception). At West Point they received instruction enabling them to obtain a degree in engineering – a skill needed in a fast-growing country – along with basic military training in the various arms. However, after graduation from the Academy there was no system of continuing advanced schooling for the individuals who would eventually rise to become general officers.

At the same time, each state had its own militia, headed by a major-general appointed by the state governor, with brigadier-generals appointed to command largely "paper" brigades. In some cases these men had military experience, but they were just as apt to be purely political appointees.

When the Civil War broke out in 1861 it was obvious that the tiny pre-war regular army could not sustain the Union's war effort alone, especially given the fact that about one-third of that army's 1,100-odd officers chose to serve the Confederacy. New brigadier- and major-generals would be needed to command the large brigades and divisions that would be formed. These men, however, would receive only temporary rank as "generals of volunteers" rather than regular army rank. In many cases regular officers serving at much lower grades offered their services to their state governors and, because of the need for men with any degree of real military experience, were directly appointed generals of volunteers. Other generals of volunteers were appointed from state militias, often because they had been important in the minority political party and the administration felt it was important to show bipartisan support for the war.

The army in the field grew so large that as early as 1862 corps were formed by assembling divisions. These corps were commanded by major-generals, there being no higher rank authorized. Indeed, major-generals also commanded the field armies, and the "general-in-chief" was a major-general until Ulysses S.Grant received an appointment as lieutenant-general, a rank re-created by Congress which had last been given to George Washington.

The performance of these generals varied tremendously. A few proved to be outstanding. Some were so abysmal that they were forced out of the service early on; while others did so well that they were offered regular army commissions (often at considerably lower ranks than those they had held during the war) at the end of hostilities. Between these two extremes we find the mass of men who proved themselves more or less competent at the head of brigades, divisions, and corps. Some who acquitted themselves well at the lower levels of command were over-promoted and seem to have been overwhelmed by their increased responsibilities. Both those who rose to the challenge well, and those who were defeated by it, included pre-war professional officers and political appointees alike.

One quality which most shared – a quality whose absence was quickly noticed, and was not tolerated, by their contemporaries – was physical courage. On the battlefields of the 1860s general officers were expected routinely to expose themselves to the dangers faced by their men, and many paid with their lives and limbs. (Of the 28 generals whose careers are described in this book, ten were wounded in action at least once and three were killed.)

George McClellan (the short figure sixth from left – he was only about 5ft.4ins. tall) meets President Abraham Lincoln after the bloody battle of Antietam in September 1862. The figure central between McClellan and Lincoln is Fitz John Porter; George A.Custer, then a subaltern on McClellan's staff, stands far right next to the tent flap, wearing a tall-crowned slouch hat.

Sherman on staffs

Each general was allowed a staff to help him exercise command. One of the Union's leading generals, William T. Sherman, wrote about staffs after the war, based on his experience:

"I don't believe in a chief of staff at all, and any general commanding an army, corps, or division, that has a staff-officer who professes to know more than his chief, is to be pitied. Every regiment should have a competent adjutant, quartermaster, and commissary, with two or three medical officers. Each brigade commander should have the same staff, with the addition of a couple of young aides-de-camp, habitually selected from the subalterns of the brigade, who should be good riders, and intelligent enough to give and explain the orders of their general.

"The same staff will answer for a division. The general in command of a separate army, and of a *corps d'armée*, should have the same professional assistance, with two or more good engineers, and his adjutant-general should exercise all the functions usually ascribed to a chief of staff, viz., he should possess the ability to comprehend the scope of operations, and to make verbally and in writing all the orders and details necessary to carry into effect the views of his general, as well as to keep the returns and records of events for the information of the next high authority, and for history. A bulky staff implies a division of responsibility, slowness of action, and indecision, whereas a small staff implies action and concentration of purpose. The smallness of General Grant's staff throughout the civil war forms the best model for future imitation."

BIOGRAPHIES: EAST

BARLOW, Francis Channing (1834–96)

Francis Channing Barlow (**see Plate F2**) was born in Brooklyn, New York, on 19 October 1834. His father was a minister, and he was raised in his mother's hometown of Brookline, Massachusetts. Barlow was a member of the Harvard graduating class of 1855, after which he went to New York to study law. Admitted to the bar in 1858, he was in practice there until the outbreak of the Civil War.

He joined the 12th Regiment, New York State Militia as a private in the heat of passion that followed the Confederate attack on Fort Sumter. The next evening, 20 April 1861, he married Arabella Griffith at St Paul's Chapel. He joined out of love of his country, and after the war he would write: "No one rejoices more than myself in the overcoming of a rebellion the design of which was to destroy this Government for the purpose of maintaining the monstrous institution of slavery."

Barlow would not remain a private for long. Within two weeks of enlisting he had been commissioned a first lieutenant in the regiment's engineer company. He was mustered out at the end of the regiment's term of three months' service; and was then appointed lieutenant-colonel of the 61st New York Infantry. One of his soldiers later wrote that Barlow "was not at first sight an impressive looking officer. He was of medium height, of slight build, with a pallid countenance, and a weakish drawling voice. In his movements there was an appearance of loose jointedness and an absence of prim stiffness."

Rapidly promoted to colonel, he led the 61st throughout the Peninsula campaign. In battle there he proved his personal heroism, and demanded the same from his soldiers. In the Seven Days' fighting (25 June–1 July 1862), at the head of his regiment as it moved up to the line, he came across several unarmed, skulking Federal soldiers. "I spoke to several and asked them why they did not go on. They said they had lost their guns," he wrote. "I pointed them out to my men as examples of what a coward is." He praised the conduct of his own men once they got into action, saying that "The greater part of the men stood firm and erect during the firing, and only stooped or went down when ordered to do so… ."

At Antietam (17 September 1862) he was severely wounded but, two days later, his service was recognised by appointment as a brigadier-general of volunteers. He was given command of a brigade in XI Corps which, at Chancellorsville (1–6 May 1863), was driven from the field in confusion during the flank attack made by Stonewall Jackson's corps on the Union right.

In the defense of Cemetery Ridge on the first day of Gettysburg (1 July 1863) Barlow was wounded and left for dead on the field, with his arms and legs temporarily paralyzed. Years after the war the Confederate Gen. John B.Gordon described how he ran across a wounded Union officer after the first day's fighting. "Quickly dismounting and lifting his head, I gave him water from my canteen, asking his name and the character of his wounds. He was Major General Francis C.Barlow, of New York, and of Howard's corps." In fact, however, modern scholarship has proved that Gordon was not in the same part of the field as Barlow, and this story was not based in fact.

Exchanged by the Confederates, Barlow recovered in time to participate in the 1864 campaign against Lee's Army of Northern Virginia as a divisional commander in II Corps under Winfield Scott Hancock. It was during this campaign, at Spotsylvania, that he decided his troops could overrun Confederate entrenchments by a massive attack in column, without artillery preparation or any halting to fire. In the early hours of 12 May 1864, somewhat delayed by fog, his division and that commanded by David Birney smashed through the Confederate lines at the "Mule Shoe", capturing some 3,000 prisoners including two generals, 30 colors, and 20 cannon.

After a forced absence on sick leave during the siege of Petersburg, Barlow recovered and returned to the army to be active at the battle of Sailor's Creek and in the Appomattox campaign. On 25 May 1865 he was named a major-general of volunteers in recognition of his service.

After the war Barlow went into politics, twice being elected secretary of state in New York, as well as serving as a United States marshal and the state attorney general in 1871. It was in this latter position that he began the first prosecution of the politically corrupt "Tweed Ring" in New York City. He died in New York on 11 January 1896, and was buried in Brookline, Massachusetts.

Engraved portrait of Francis Barlow from the 9 July 1864 issue of *Harper's Weekly*. He wears a somewhat oversized custom-made fatigue blouse or "sack coat", with the single star of a brigadier-general on the front of his forage cap. According to to the paper, "Throughout the [1864] campaign Barlow is conspicious among the noble band of united heroes, officers and men, in the very active front of the battle." Badly wounded at both Antietam and Gettysburg, this pale, slightly built 30-year-old gained his greatest success in the capture of the "Mule Shoe" salient at Spotsylvania in May 1864.

BURNSIDE, Ambrose Everett (1824–81)

Ambrose Burnside (**see Plate C2**) was born at Liberty, Indiana, on 23 May 1824. After finishing primary school he was apprenticed to a tailor, and later became a partner in a tailor's shop in Liberty before his father was able to secure him an appointment to the US Military Academy. He was graduated from the Academy in 1847 and appointed a brevet second lieutenant in the 2nd Artillery.

As the war in Mexico was nearly finished when he graduated, his only wartime service was in the Mexico City garrison. Thereafter he served on the southwestern frontier, being wounded slightly in a skirmish with Apaches in 1849. While in the army he invented a breech-loading carbine which used a fixed brass cartridge. He resigned his commission in 1853 and went to Bristol, Rhode Island, where he gathered investors to begin manufacturing this weapon. He was, however, unable to sell it to the army. A very sociable man, Burnside was both nominated to Congress and given a job with the Illinois Central Railroad, then being run by George B.McClellan, an old army friend. Burnside also became major-general of the Rhode Island militia.

On the outbreak of war Burnside organised the 1st Rhode Island Infantry, one of the first northern regiments to march to the relief of Washington. He was there given command of a brigade, which he commanded at First Bull Run (21 July 1861). For his service he received a commission as brigadier-general of volunteers on 6 August. Burnside was friendly with President Lincoln, and received command of the expedition sent to the North Carolina coast, where he successfully made landings and set up permanent bases. For these successes he was promoted to major-general of volunteers on 18 March 1862.

Returning to the Army of the Potomac outside Washington, Burnside was given command of IX Corps at Antietam. During the battle of 17 September 1862 he moved slowly, taking precious hours to capture a bridge across Antietam Creek, which could have been forded easily at a number of points; this delay allowed Lee to concentrate his troops to face other threats. Even so, when McClellan was relieved of command for not pursuing Lee, Lincoln appointed Burnside to command the Army of the Potomac on 7 November 1862.

The army, loyal to McClellan from top to bottom, was not happy about the change. Major-General Marsena Patrick, the army's provost marshal, wrote that after Burnside took over "He appeared well – very well, but all seemed to think there was one they liked much better… ." Patrick also observed that Burnside was "rather obtuse in his conceptions & is very forgetful."

Burnside led the Army of the Potomac directly south toward Richmond, but was halted on the Rappahannock River at Fredericksburg. Losing time while pontoon bridges were brought up and

Ambrose Burnside, a West Point graduate, invented a carbine, and had left the army to organize its manufacture in Rhode Island before the war broke out. He raised a regiment immediately, which became the 1st Rhode Island, and led it to Washington, where he was soon promoted to a brigade command. Here he wears his original regimental uniform, a dark blue overshirt with gray trousers; it is intriguing to recall that his first trade was as a tailor.

emplaced, he then ordered his army into repeated frontal charges against Confederate positions on higher ground which Lee had been able to prepare while awaiting the attack (13 December 1862). The attempt was a total and very costly failure; nevertheless, Burnside wanted to lead his own IX Corps in renewed attacks the next day, finally being talked out of it by his subordinates.

He then started to move the army west along the Rappahannock to outflank Lee; but the weather turned against him, and the Army of the Potomac became mired in the mud. Unable to move, Burnside then asked Lincoln either to relieve him or to dismiss some troublesome subordinates; and the President chose to replace him with Joseph Hooker.

Burnside received command of the Department of the Ohio in March 1863, ably defending Knoxville, Tennessee, against Confederate attack – though Patrick noted, "We may look for any disaster from Burnside. He is unfit to be in any separate command."

IX Corps was brought up to strength, and Burnside resumed command and rejoined the Army of the Potomac, although directly under command of the overall army commander, U.S. Grant, for the 1864 campaign that led to the siege of Petersburg. There he proposed a disastrous attempt on Confederate lines following a huge mine explosion ("the Crater", 30 July 1864) – a mismanaged attack which cost enormous casualties. Burnside resigned on 15 April 1865.

After the war he was elected governor of Rhode Island three times, and thereafter as one of the state's senators, in which position he was serving at his death on 13 September 1881.

BUTLER, Benjamin Franklin (1818–93)

Born in Deerfield, New Hampshire on 5 November 1818, Butler (see Plate A2) graduated from Colby College in Maine in 1838. Returning to Lowell, he was admitted to the bar in 1840 and practiced criminal law as well as entering politics. He was elected to the Massachusetts legislature in 1853 and again in 1859, serving as a representative to the Democratic Convention. He endorsed Southern rights, being a supporter of the extreme States' Rights candidate, John C.Breckinridge.

Despite this position, Butler – a brigadier-general in theMassachusetts militia before the war – led his 8th Massachusetts Regiment to Washington in 1861. There, on 16 May, he was appointed a major-general of volunteers, more to indicate proof of Democratic support for putting down the Southern "rebellion" than as a testimony to his abilities. Sent to Fortress Monroe, Butler led an expedition that was defeated at Big Bethel (10 June), the first noted Union defeat of the war.

The sociable and popular Burnside, here wearing regulation uniform as a major-general, became the Army of the Potomac's third commander, but – as he freely admitted – he lacked the ability for such a post. After greatly damaging the army at Fredericksburg he was demoted to command of his old IX Corps. After the war Ulysses S.Grant wrote of him: "General Burnside was an officer who was generally liked and respected. He was not, however, fitted to command an army. No one knew this better than himself. He always admitted his blunders, and extenuated those of officers under him beyond what they were entitled to. It was hardly his fault that he was ever assigned to a separate command."

"I regret that he has not as much capacity for handling troops judiciously in the field as he has for 'managing' his superiors and kicking out his subordinates", wrote Brig.Gen. Joseph R.Hawley, who later served under Butler. "Yet I wish that some of our accomplished soldiers had some of his peculiar traits, & his knowledge of men & things generally crowded into their somewhat narrow professional minds."

While at Monroe, Butler ruled that slaves who escaped to Union lines did not have to be returned to their owners, since their use aided the Confederates and they were thus "contraband of war". Such sinuous legal reasoning was typical of the man; one of his officers would write, "Butler is sharp, shrewd, able, without conscience or modesty – overbearing. A bad man to have against you in a criminal case." Another of his officers called him astute, quick-witted, unscrupulous, and audacious. Some of his actions at Monroe were certainly questionable. He sold trade permits to civilians who did business in his department. He received kickbacks from Northern firms that sold farm implements and other goods to Southern companies that could pay in cotton. Some of this cotton may have been shipped north in army transports, loaded by army troops and stevedores.

In August 1861 Butler was sent with a force to take Hatteras Inlet, which he did successfully. In May 1862 he commanded the troops that took over New Orleans after the US Navy forced its surrender. There he ruled that women who

Benjamin Butler had been involved in the Massachusetts militia before the war, but his main interests lay in politics. It was his considerable Democrat powerbase in New England which brought him appointment as a major-general, but he proved a poor commander. It was only after the 1864 presidential election, however, when the Republicans were safely in office and the Confederacy appeared doomed, that the government felt safe in dismissing him. Note the oakleaf embroidery on his collar, a personal affectation.

BELOW This engraving from a photograph shows Butler wearing another heavily embroidered uniform, recalling that worn by Winfield Scott. Always a political animal, and widely suspected of corruption, Butler made friends with the press correspondents accompanying the army, being especially helpful to those who gave him favorable coverage. However, a positive consequence of his self-seeking character was that he also made sure that his soldiers were on his side by expediting mail to and from the front, as well as aiding the US Sanitary Commission and US Christian Commission in their work for the troops – his commands were noted for having among the best, most forward hospital facilities.

insulted Union officers were to be treated as women of the night plying their trade. The South was deeply insulted by this order, and actually placed a price on Butler's head. There, too, he gained the nickname of "Spoons Butler", it being said that he stole silver spoons, as well as other personal property, for his own benefit. Such allegations were not proved, but he was relieved of command there in December 1862.

In 1864 Butler was named commander of a new Army of the James, made up of several corps drawn from the deep South. This was intended to land at Bermuda Hundred and take Richmond from the south. In fact Confederate forces managed to entrench in his front, and those works, coupled with his indecision, halted his force as if he had been corked in a bottle. He then led a force against Fort Fisher, the last fort in the Confederacy to defend an Atlantic Coast port; this attempt failed after his plan to explode a ship full of powder did not level the fort as expected. He was recalled to New York in November 1864, and in January 1865 he was forced to resign his commission.

After Butler was gone the army appointed a commission to look into charges of corruption against him. The report they produced indicated that Butler was indeed involved in such activities, but nothing happened as a result.

Changing his affiliation to Republican, Butler was elected to Congress between 1866 and 1875 and again in 1878 (this time as a "Greenbacker"), and was elected governor in 1882. He was the Greenbacker presidential candidate in 1884, and died in Washington, DC on 11 January 1893.

CHAMBERLAIN, Joshua Lawrence (1828–1919)

Born in Brewer, Maine, on 8 September 1828, Chamberlain (**see Plate H3**) was educated at a military academy at Ellsworth, then graduated from Bowdoin College in 1852; finally he graduated from the Bangor Theological Seminary in 1855. He was then named a professor at Bowdoin, the post that he held when the Civil War began.

Commissioned lieutenant-colonel of the 20th Maine in August 1862, he subsequently became the unit's colonel. Given his military academy and teaching experience, he seems to have been well regarded in the regiment. Major Holman Melcher wrote home on 27 June 1863 that "Our beloved Col. Chamberlain is not able to command us owing to sickness, but he is on the recovery and we all hail the day he is able to resume his command of the regiment."

Joshua Chamberlain saw active service from Antietam to Appomattox; but it was 2 July 1863, the second day of Gettysburg, that brought him his most famous moment. Vincent's brigade was hurried to hold a position at the far left of the Union line, and the 20th Maine was posted on the extreme left of the brigade – and thus of the whole Union army – with orders to hold the commanding height of Little Round Top. Law's Alabama brigade moved against them, and Chamberlain's men held off assault after assault. Finally, with the regiment's ammunition exhausted, Chamberlain called for a bayonet assault, leading it down the hill in person against the weary Confederates (who, in fact, were preparing to retire as the 20th's charge hit them). For this action, after the war, Chamberlain was awarded the Medal of Honor. Chamberlain described his defense of Little Round Top in a letter to Maine's governor on 21 July 1863:

"We were assigned to the *extreme left* of our line of battle, where the fiercest assault was made. A whole Rebel Brigade was opposed to this Regiment, charging on us with desperate fury, in column of Regiments, so that we had to contend with a front of *fresh troops* after each struggle. After two hours fighting on the defensive, our loss had been so great, & the remaining men were so much exhausted, having fired all our 'sixty-rounds' & all the cartridges we could gather from the scattered boxes of the fallen around us, friend & foe, I saw no way left but to take the *offensive* & accordingly we charged on the enemy – trying 'cold steel' on them. The result was we drove them entirely out of the field, killing one hundred & fifty of them & taking *three hundred & eight* prisoners & two hundred & seventy five stand of arms."

Although not wounded at Gettysburg, in all Chamberlain would be wounded six times during the war. Later a brigade commander, he saw heavy action in the 1864 campaign against the Army of Northern Virginia. While leading his men in an attack against Petersburg he was seriously – indeed, it was believed mortally – wounded by a bullet that passed through his lower right abdomen. He was given a field promotion to brigadier-general; as Grant later described it, "Colonel J.L. Chamberlain, of the 20th Maine, was wounded on the 18th. He was gallantly leading his brigade at the time, as he had been in the habit of doing in all the engagements in which he had previously been engaged. He had several time been recommended for a brigadier-generalcy for gallant and meritorious conduct. On this occasion, however, I promoted him on the spot, and forwarded a copy of my order to the War Department, asking that my act might be confirmed and Chamberlain's name sent to the Senate for confirmation without any delay. This was done... ."

Despite continual pain from his wound, which never did heal completely, Chamberlain returned to the front in November 1864. At Five Forks (1 April 1865) he was breveted a major-general for his conduct; and a week later it was to Chamberlain that Gen. Grant gave the honor of receiving the formal surrender of the Army of Northern Virginia at Appomattox.

After the war he was offered a regular army commission, but declined it and was mustered out in January 1866. Returning to Maine, he was elected governor of the state, a post he won in two following elections. After leaving office in 1870 he returned to Bowdoin to become the college's president, also lecturing in political science and public law. He did maintain his military interests, however, serving as major-general of Maine's militia. He also had business interests in Florida, as well as serving as surveyor of the port of Portland, Maine; and he wrote about the war. He died at Portland in his 91st year, on 24 February 1919, as a long-delayed consequence of his Civil War wounds.

COUCH, Darius Nash (1832–97)

Darius Couch (**see Plate D2**) was born in Putnam County, New York, on 23 July 1832. A graduate of West Point in 1842, he was sent to the Mexican War with Company B, 4th US Artillery. There he took ill from severe intestinal dysentery which, coupled with the rheumatic fever from which he also appears to have suffered, virtually crippled him at various times throughout the rest of his life. Couch recovered in time to see his first action at Buena Vista (22–23 February 1847), of which he wrote that

This engraving of Darius Couch was made from a photograph taken when he was still a brigadier-general. Often ill following service in the far South as a young officer, he declined the chance to become commander of the Army of the Potomac during the Gettysburg campaign instead of Meade.

Couch was something of an intellectual; he had taken leave from the army after the Seminole War, pursuing field research into the flora and fauna of northern Mexico for the Smithsonian Institution, and in 1852 he discovered a species of platyfish which was named in his honor, *Xiphophorus couchiana*.

he saw "plenty signs of the battle. Wounded men who had crawled to a cover, horses likewise without their masters, stragglers behind bushes, etc, the dead and dying lying side by side. I nerved myself in the sight and looked on unmoved."

Breveted a first lieutenant for his gallant conduct in this battle, Couch subsequently saw service in the Seminole War (1849–50), for which he was commended by the Secretary of War. He resigned his commission in 1855 to marry, and joined a copper manufacturing business run by his father-in-law in Taunton, Massachusetts. This was a period when many dedicated officers despaired of a career in the tiny, cash-starved peacetime army, where promotion was desperately slow even for men of proven merit.

When the Civil War broke out, Couch was authorized by the state governor to raise the 7th Massachusetts Infantry, which he led to Washington in July 1861. He was quickly appointed a brigadier-general of volunteers and given a brigade command. When the Army of the Potomac began the Peninsula campaign (April–May 1862) he commanded the 1st Division, IV Corps. "It was a miserably fought affair," he wrote of his first battle in the campaign, at Williamsburg; "… a few thousand Confederates held us all in check seeing that our people went in by driblets." Couch's disillusionment with the army commander, George McClellan, deepened during the Seven Days, when he complained that "we commenced falling back at 11pm leaving many gallant men desperately wounded and in the enemy's hands… a perfect rout… the same soldiers that had fought so magnificently during the last seven days were now a mob."

Suffering from one of his recurrent bouts of illness, Couch offered to resign after these battles, but his resignation was not accepted and he went on sick leave. In September 1862 he was back in command of a division and, on 7 November 1862, of II Corps. He led his corps at Fredericksburg (13 December 1862), where he argued against Burnside's plan of attack. Subsequently the second in command of the army under Hooker, Couch found himself in effective command at Chancellorsville (1–6 May 1863) when the latter was stunned by the turn of events. Couch ably organized a defense, stabilizing the front after it had apparently fallen apart, and was twice wounded.

While he was on sick leave after Chancellorsville he met Lincoln, who offered him command of the Army of the Potomac, but he declined for health reasons, instead suggesting George Meade. Couch was then named to command the Department of the Susquehanna – right in the path of Lee's invasion of Pennsylvania, which was part of his department. Couch disagreed with state politicians during the campaign, and afterwards was sent to command the 2nd Division, XXIII Corps at Nashville, Tennessee, where he saw much action. The end of the war found him in North

Carolina; resigning his commission on 9 June 1865, he returned home, where he ran unsuccessfully for governor of Massachusetts. After this defeat he moved to Connecticut, where he became the state's adjutant general. Couch died at Norwalk in February 1897.

CUSTER, George Armstrong (1839–76)

George Custer was born on 5 December 1839 in New Rumley, Ohio. While a teacher in Ohio he was appointed to West Point in 1857. Graduating last in his class of 1861, he was then assigned as a staff officer in the Army of the Potomac. He distinguished himself several times while holding the brevet rank of captain on the staffs of George B. McClellan and Alfred Pleasonton, and at the age of only 23 was appointed a brigadier-general of volunteers on 29 June 1863. He was assigned to command a brigade of Michigan cavalry in Judson Kilpatrick's division, first leading it at Gettysburg a few days later. Colonel J.H.Kidd, 6th Michigan Cavalry, later described the new brigadier:

"George A.Custer was, as all agree, the most picturesque figure of the civil war… Brave but not reckless; self-confident, yet modest; ambitious, but regulating his conduct at all times by a high sense of honor and duty; eager for laurels, but scorning to wear them unworthily; ready and willing to act… quick in emergencies, cool and self-possessed, his courage was of the highest moral type, his perceptions were intuitions… He was not a reckless commander. He was not regardless of human life… He was kind to his subordinates, tolerant of their weaknesses, always ready to help and encourage them. He was brave as a lion, fought as few men fought, but it was from no love of it."

Kidd also described his appearance: "An officer superbly mounted who sat his charger as if to the manor born. Tall, lithe, active, muscular, straight as an Indian and as quick in his movements, he had the fair complexion of a school girl. He was clad in a suit of black velvet, elaborately trimmed with gold lace, which ran down the outer seams of his trousers, and almost covered the sleeves of his cavalry jacket. The wide collar of a blue navy shirt was turned down over the collar of his velvet jacket, and a necktie of brilliant crimson was tied in a graceful knot at the throat, the long ends falling carelessly in front. The double rows of buttons on his breast were arranged in groups of twos, indicating the rank of brigadier-general. A soft, black hat with wide brim adorned with a gilt cord, and rosette encircling a silver star, was worn turned down on one side giving him a rakish air. His golden hair fell in

15

graceful luxuriance nearly or quite to his shoulders, and his upper lip was garnished with a blonde mustache. A sword and belt, gilt spurs and top boots completed his unique outfit." He further admitted that "Custer with flashing eye and flowing hair, charging at the head of his men, was a grand and picturesque figure, the more so by reason of his fantastic uniform, which made him a conspicuous mark for the enemy's bullets, but a coward in Custer's uniform would have become the laughing stock of the army."

Made a major-general of volunteers after Appomattox, he reverted to lieutenant-colonel on the regular army list after the war, assigned to the 7th Cavalry. Court-martialed for being absent without leave, and unwise in his public pronouncements, he was nevertheless restored to duty and took part in the 1867 campaign against the Sioux and Cheyenne; the Yellowstone Expedition of 1873; the expedition into the Black Hills in 1874; and the Cheyenne and Sioux campaign of 1876. It was during a detached march in this latter campaign that he divided his regiment in the face of a much larger Indian force at the Little Big Horn on 25 June 1876, in which action he and all the men under his personal command lost their lives.

FRANKLIN, William Buel (1823–1903)

William Franklin **(see Plate D3)** was born on 27 February 1823 at York, Pennsylvania. Ranked first in the West Point class of 1843 (in which U.S. Grant ranked 21st), he was commissioned into the Corps of Topographical Engineers. He took part in the Great Lakes survey and explorations in the Rocky Mountains. In the Mexican War he earned a brevet for bravery at Buena Vista.

From 1848 to 1852 he was an assistant professor at West Point; between 1852 and the Civil War he was in Washington, where he was in charge of building the Capitol dome and the monolithic Treasury addition. On the outbreak of the Civil War he was commissioned colonel of the 12th US Infantry, and shortly thereafter a brigadier-general of volunteers on 17 May 1861. He commanded a brigade at First Bull Run (21 July), and was given a divisional command that September. He served in this capacity in the Peninsula campaign (April–May 1862), during which he was given command of VI Corps. McClellan complained to his wife in August 1862 that Franklin showed "little energy", adding "I do not at all doubt Franklin's loyalty now, but his efficiency is very little – I am very sorry that it has turned out so. The main, perhaps the only cause is that he has been & still is sick – & one ought not to judge harshly a person in that condition."

Nevertheless, leading his corps with distinction, Franklin commanded the troops at Crampton's Gap at South Mountain (14 September 1862), and three days later fought at Antietam. Burnside picked him to command the Left Grand Division, consisting of I and VI Corps, at Fredericksburg that December. Franklin was bitter about Burnside's botched attack: "Both his staff and Smith's are talking outrageously, only repeating though, no doubt, the words of their generals," wrote Charles Wainwright after the battle. "Burnside may be unfit to command this army; his present plan may be absurd, and failure certain; but his lieutenants have no right to say so to their subordinates. As it is, Franklin has talked so much and so loudly to this effect ever since the present move was decided on, that he has completely demoralized his whole command, and so rendered failure doubly sure. His conduct has been such that he certainly deserves to be broken."

Burnside wanted Franklin removed from command, but Lincoln refused; instead he accepted Burnside's resignation. Marsena Patrick reported the rumor going through the army on 11 January 1863: "The contest is between Franklin & Hooker for the succession." Eventually, however, he had to record on 28 January that "Gen. Franklin was ordered to turn over the Command of the grand Division & report in Washington. Many persons think it is probable that Franklin will have a trial. Undoubtedly there is a great deal of disloyalty, according to Judge Holt's interpretation of that word, in Franklin's command."

William Buel Franklin as a major-general – a *Harper's Weekly* engraving after a Brady photograph. Academically one of the most distinguished of all Union general officers, he graduated top of his class at West Point and became a celebrated engineer. His high reputation saved his career when his outspoken criticism of superiors brought him into serious disfavor.

Franklin was not court-martialed; Capt. Charles Francis Adams Jr, 1st Massachusetts Cavalry, wrote that Franklin was "on the whole considered the ablest officer we have," and such a reputation may have saved him. However, he was not restored at once to a senior command. After some months he was given XIX Corps in the West, during both the Sabine Pass expedition and the Red River campaign (March–May 1864); he was wounded during the latter. At the end of the war Franklin was named president of the board for retiring disabled officers. However, his outspokenness against Burnside had so turned his fellow generals against him that he resigned his commission in 1866.

After the war Franklin served as vice-president and general manager of Colt's Fire Arms Manufacturing Co. until 1888. During that time he also supervised the building of the Connecticut state capitol, and was a Democratic presidential elector in the 1876 election. He was named commissioner general of the United States for the Paris Exposition in 1888. Returning to Connecticut, he died there on 8 March 1903, and is buried at York, Pennsylvania.

FRENCH, William Henry (1815–81)

William French was born on 13 January 1815 in Baltimore, Maryland. He was graduated with West Point's class of 1837, a classmate of John Sedgwick and Joseph Hooker, and assigned to the 1st US Artillery. He served in Florida and then in the Mexican War, where he was breveted a captain and a major for gallantry and meritorious conduct.

The outbreak of the Civil War found him in command of a garrison deep in Southern territory, at Eagle Pass, Texas. Rather than surrender to state authorities, he marched his men to the mouth of the Rio Grande and then embarked on boats to go to Key West, still under Federal authority. He was then appointed a brigadier-general of volunteers, ranking from 28 September 1861, and given a command in II Corps during the Peninsula campaign (April–May 1862). On 4 June 1862, Charles Haydon, an officer in the 2nd Michigan, recorded French being introduced to his command as a general "who greatly distinguished himself at Fair Oaks… He was cheered beyond measure. There is no doubt that he is one of the best fighting Generals in the army." With this reputation, French went on to be a division commander at Antietam that September, promoted to major-general on 29 November 1862. He continued in this command at Fredericksburg and Chancellorsville (December 1862 and May 1863), thereafter being transferred to command the District of Harper's Ferry.

After Chancellorsville, French succeeded to the command of III Corps. However, he was blamed for much of the failure of the Mine Run campaign in November 1863, especially by Meade. Marsena Patrick noted in his diary on 26 November that the army was delayed by the slowness of French's corps to move, adding, "Meade was very angry (& justly) at this terrible delay and carelessness… ." French was a stout and red-faced individual, and there was talk that his problems were caused by alcohol. He compounded his misfortune when his corps accidentally ran into the Confederates and brought on an engagement. "The blame for the failure is pretty generally laid upon General French," Charles Wainwright recorded on 29 November, adding on 10 December that the campaign's failure "was no doubt mainly owing to General French, who

I find it generally believed was drunk. I cannot vouch for the truth of this, however, and hope it was not so. He certainly lost his way twice, and appears to have acted very queerly."

French was aware of this muttering, and apparently fed misleading information to a correspondent with the *New York Herald*, which printed stories praising French's command. "It seems to be the idea," Patrick wrote on 6 December, "that this fellow is employed by French & his Clique, to forestall public opinion & set up French, before 'Official' papers are made public."

Perhaps these stories did their intended work. Indeed, there was even some talk that French, then senior corps commander in the Army of the Potomac, might be picked by the newly arriving U.S.Grant to replace Meade as army commander. This did not happen, however; French continued in his command until III Corps, much shrunken by the end of enlistments in the spring of 1864, was merged into another command. French was mustered out of volunteer service with effect from 6 May 1864. He served on various military boards until the end of the war, by which time he held the rank of colonel in command of the 4th US Artillery. He retired in 1880 and died in Washington on 20 May 1881, being buried in Rock Creek Cemetery.

GIBBON, John (1827–96)
Born in Philadelphia, Pennsylvania, on 20 April 1827, John Gibbon (**see Plate F3**) was graduated from the US Military Academy in 1847. He saw service in Mexico and in the Seminole War, and as an artillery instructor at West Point, writing a standard book on the subject thereafter. On the

George McClellan and Lincoln meet privately after Antietam in the fall of 1862. The president desperately wanted McClellan to resume the offensive, but the ever-cautious general continued to stall. When it was reported that the army's horses were worn out, Lincoln asked what on earth they'd done to *get* worn out?

When John Gibbon, a professional artilleryman, first earned command of an infantry brigade, contemporaries predicted that the unit would not be drilled in evolutions of the line, known only by infantry officers. Gibbon, however, bought and memorized a manual and astonished his peers with his well-drilled brigade. His command would become famous as the "Iron Brigade" of mid-Western troops, known by their Hardee hats – one of Gibbon's innovations to improve morale. At about the time of Gettysburg, the staff officer Frank Haskell described him as "compactly made, neither spare nor corpulent, with ruddy complexion, chestnut brown hair, with a clean-shaved face, except his moustache, which is decidedly reddish in color, medium-sized, well-shaped head, sharp, moderately-jutting brow, deep blue, calm eyes, sharp, slightly aquiline nose, compressed mouth, full jaws and chin, with an air of calm firmness in his manner. He always looks well dressed."

When this portrait was taken he was clearly in the early stages of growing what became a full beard.

outbreak of the Civil War he found himself – like so many other officers – in a difficult position; he had spent much of his youth in North Carolina, where his parents, who owned slaves, still lived, and his wife was from Baltimore, Maryland.

While he was serving at Camp Floyd, Utah, during the uncertain period between Lincoln's election and the Confederate firing on Fort Sumter, one evening the post band struck up *Dixie*, the Southern song, shortly after the band leader received a whispered message from Gibbon's small daughter. Some officers present at the incident wrote a letter to the Secretary of War claiming to uncover a pro-Southern plot and naming Gibbon as a Southern sympathizer. On learning this Gibbon wrote a heated letter to the Adjutant General denying these charges; he demanded a court-martial, which was convened on 5 July. After a one-day session Gibbon was cleared of charges. As a firm believer in the oath he had sworn to defend his country's Constitution and obey the officers of her army, rather than following the political agenda of any particular state, Gibbon was firmly in the Union camp.

He was named chief of artillery of Irvin McDowell's division until appointed a brigadier-general of volunteers on 2 May 1862. He was given command of the only brigade of troops from Western states, a hard-fighting unit that won the nickname of the "Iron Brigade". There he was described by one of his officers as "bland and genial," while another said he was "a plain, common man, [who] will listen to the complaint of a private as soon as he will to a colonel." Gibbon relied on incentives rather than punishment to maintain discipline. To improve morale he adopted the US Army's dress uniform, with added gaiters, for his brigade's field dress. On the other hand, no commander can ever be universally admired: one of his Wisconsin soldiers called him "a manufactured aristocrat, who owes all his importance to the circumstances that created him," adding that he was "arbitrary, severe and exacting… distant, formal and reserved."

In November 1862, Gibbon was given command of the 2nd Division, I Corps. Badly wounded at Fredericksburg (13 December 1862), he returned to duty after three months' recuperation. He was then placed in command of the 2nd Division of II Corps. In this appointment he was wounded once more at Gettysburg (1–3 July 1863).

After recovering again, Gibbon was given command of draft depots in Cleveland and Philadelphia. With the start of the 1864 campaign he returned to the Army of the Potomac, fighting with distinction at the head of his old division. He was promoted major-general ranking from 7 June 1864. In January 1865 he was given command of XXIV Corps in the Army of the James. He was one of the commissioners named to receive the surrender of the Army of Northern Virginia at Appomattox.

After the war Gibbon was named colonel on the regular army roster in command of the 36th US Infantry, transferring to the 7th US Infantry in 1869. He was involved in the 1876 campaign against the Sioux, followed by the Nez Perces campaign. He was named a brigadier-general in the regular army on 10 July 1885, and retired in 1891. Serving as commander in chief of the Military Order of the Loyal Legion, a veteran officers' organization, he died in Baltimore on 6 February 1896.

HANCOCK, Winfield Scott (1824–86)

Winfield Scott Hancock (see Plate F1) was born, one of twins, on 14 February 1824 near Norristown, Pennsylvania, where he is buried today. He was graduated towards the bottom of the West Point class of 1844, and was assigned to the infantry. He served in the Mexican War, winning a brevet for gallantry; in the Kansas War against the Seminoles; and in the Utah expedition. When the Civil War broke out he was chief quartermaster in the sleepy southern California town of Los Angeles. Returning east, he was immediately named a brigadier-general of volunteers, dating from 23 September 1861. As a brigade commander he served in the Army of the Potomac in the Peninsula campaign of April–May 1862.

It was on the Peninsula that he gained his nickname, when the army's commander telegraphed his wife with news of the day's battle, adding that "Hancock was superb". The dispatch found its way into print, and thereafter he was always "Hancock the Superb." The staff officer Frank Haskell afterwards wrote that Hancock was "the most magnificent looking General in the whole Army of the Potomac… the tallest and most shapely, and in many respects the best looking officer of them all. His hair is very light brown, straight and moist, and always looks well, his beard is of the same color, of which he wears the moustache and a tuft under the chin; complexion ruddy, features neither large nor small, but well cut, with full jaw and chin, compressed mouth, straight nose, full, deep blue eyes, and a very mobile, emotional countenance. He always dresses remarkably well, and his manner is dignified, gentlemanly and commanding. I think if he were in citizen's

21

Hancock, commander of II Corps, stands at left center with his hand on a tree. Francis Barlow, his jacket open to show a checked shirt, leans on the same tree; while John Gibbon is the third man to the right of Hancock, hatless, leaning on his sword, and wearing a single-breasted sack coat. Cf Plate F.

clothes, and should give commands in the army to those who did not know him, he would be likely to be obeyed at once, and without any question as to his right to command."

In September 1862 Hancock took his men into the Antietam campaign, and when Maj.Gen.Israel B.Richardson was mortally wounded he succeeded him in command of the 1st Division, II Corps; he formally received the rank of major-general of volunteers on 29 November 1862. He distinguished himself thereafter at Fredericksburg (December 1862), and after Chancellorsville (May 1863) his division covered the retreat of the Union army across the Rappahannock.

When he arrived on the field of Gettysburg on 1 July 1863 Hancock found I and XI Corps badly beaten, and immediately took command. He drew up a defensive line based on Cemetery Ridge, advising the army's new commander, Meade, to fight on this field rather than withdraw. Two days later, when the Confederates – led by such old friends of his as Lewis Armistead and Richard B.Garnett – struck his troops during Pickett's Charge, he was badly wounded when a bullet tore into his saddle, sending pieces of wood and a nail into his thigh. For a while his condition was cause for serious concern, but he recovered by the end of 1863 and was able to return to command II Corps.

Many of the senior figures in the Army of the Potomac were convinced that Hancock would succeed Meade as the army commander, but Grant retained Meade and kept Hancock as a corps commander. He led his corps in all the battles up to Petersburg in summer 1864, winning Grant's appreciation and promotion to the regular army rank of brigadier-general on 12 August. After the war Grant wrote:

"Hancock stands the most conspicuous figure of all the general officers who did not exercise a separate command. He commanded a corps longer than any other one, and his name was never mentioned as having committed in battle a blunder for which he was responsible. He was a man of very conspicuous personal appearance. Tall, well-formed and, at the time of which I now write, young and fresh-looking, he presented an appearance that would attract the attention of an army as he passed. His genial disposition made him friends, and his personal courage and his presence with his command in the thickest of the fight won for him the confidence of troops serving under him. No matter how hard the fight, [II Corps] always felt that their commander was looking after them."

When his Gettysburg wound reopened in November 1864 he was sent back to Washington to form a Veteran Reserve Corps, but this was only partially created. He was also given department command in February 1865, staying in that position until the end of the war. He was given command of the Department of the East in 1877, and while holding the appointment ran in the presidential election against James A.Garfield, who only narrowly beat him. Hancock died while still department commander on 9 February 1886.

HOOKER, Joseph (1814–79)

Joseph Hooker (see Plate D1) was born in Hadley, Massachusetts on 13 November 1814. After early education at Hopkins Academy in Hadley he went on to West Point, from where he was graduated in 1837. He served on various staffs during the Mexican War, winning brevets for all ranks up to that of lieutenant-colonel for his gallant and meritorious conduct. His permanent captaincy was given him in 1848, and he went on to serve as assistant adjutant general of the Pacific Division. Going on leave of absence in 1851, he resigned his commission in 1853 and took up farming near Sonoma, California.

Seeking a return to the army, Hooker was named a brigadier-general of volunteers in August 1861, and commanded a division of III Corps in the Peninsula campaign the following year. It was during this period that a newspaper headed one of its stories from the front, "Fighting – Joe Hooker"; thereafter he was known as "Fighting Joe Hooker", which he found embarrassing. He commanded his division and then I Corps in the Seven Days' Battles of June–July 1862, at Second Bull Run (Manassas) in August, and Antietam in September. At Fredericksburg that December he was given command of two corps as the Center Grand Division. His criticisms of Burnside during this campaign caused the latter to request his removal; but Lincoln chose to appoint him commander of the Army of the Potomac in Burnside's stead.

"Fighting Joe" Hooker – an accidental and, as it turned out, perhaps inappropriate nickname – had sandy hair and pale blue eyes. Hooker had a weakness for the ladies and his headquarters swarmed with them; as a result a certain class of women became known as "hookers", a term still in use today.

23

Hooker (front, second from right) with his staff. Whatever his failings in the field, he greatly improved morale in the Army of the Potomac after Fredericksburg with a combination of furloughs, dress parades, more clothes and equipment, and more food.

Colonel Charles Wainwright noted in his diary in May 1862 that "General Hooker has been of the pleasantest kind, and I have him a delightful man to serve with. I do not, however, like the way he has of always decrying the other generals of his own rank, whose every act he seems to find fault with." When Hooker was named army commander Wainwright went on to write: "His bravery is unquestioned, but he has not so far shown himself anything of a tactician, and at Williamsburg he certainly did not appear to be master of the situation. One great quality I think he has, a good judgment of men to serve under him. I am asked on all sides here if he drinks. Though thrown in very close contact with him through six months, I never saw him when I thought him the worse for liquor. Indeed, I should say that his failing was more in the way of women than whiskey." John Gibbon felt that "A great deal of his attractive frankness was assumed and he was essentially an intriguer. In his intrigues, he sacrificed his soldierly principles whenever such sacrifice could gain him political influence to further his own ends."

Hooker planned a flank move around Lee, moving west and crossing the Rappahannock, cutting rapidly through the Wilderness area, and hitting Lee where he would have to attack, between Fredericksburg and Richmond. Upon reaching the area, however, he apparently lost all resolve, and had his forces pull back to defensive lines around Chancellorsville. There Lee threw in a flank move of his own, and at dusk on 2 May 1863 Stonewall Jackson smashed through Hooker's right. Hooker's apparent paralysis of will persisted, and only the accidental death of Jackson, and hard fighting by Hooker's subordinates, saved the Union army from a worse disaster.

Relieved of command as Lee headed north into Pennsylvania two months later, Hooker was sent to the West with the ill-fated XI and XII Corps, later consolidated into XX Corps. There he fought quite well under command of U.S.Grant at Chattanooga in October 1863. After the war Grant wrote:

"Of Hooker I saw but little during the war. I had known him very well before, however. Where I did see him, at Chattanooga, his achievement in bringing his command around the point of Lookout Mountain and into Chattanooga Valley was brilliant. I nevertheless regarded him as a dangerous man. He was not subordinate to his superiors. He was ambitious to the extent of caring nothing for the rights of others. His disposition was, when engaged in battle, to get detached from the main body of the army and exercise a separate command, gathering to his standard all he could of his juniors."

After James McPherson was killed at Atlanta, Oliver O.Howard, who was subordinate to Hooker, was named to command the Army of Tennessee. Hooker, who held rank as a brigadier-general in the regular army and major-general of volunteers, asked to be relieved from "an army in which rank and service are ignored." Sherman let him go, and he only held a departmental command until he retired in 1868. He died in Garden City, New York, on 31 October 1879.

HUMPHREYS, Andrew Atkinson (1810–83)

Andrew Humphreys (**see Plate H1**) was born in Philadelphia on 2 November 1810, to a family of naval architects and constructors. After graduation from West Point in 1831 he was assigned to the Corps of Topographical Engineers, spending much of his time on hydrographical surveys of the Mississippi Delta until the Civil War broke out.

Assigned to the staff of George McClellan, commander of the Army of the Potomac, in 1861, Humphreys was named a brigadier-general of volunteers in April 1862. He served during the Peninsula campaign as the army's chief topographical engineer, a post well fitted for his methodical and precise character. In September 1862 he was given command of a newly recruited division in V Corps, which he quickly brought to a high state of combat readiness. Colonel Charles Wainwright noted at Fredericksburg that December that "Humphreys's division of entirely new troops quite rivaled the old Second Corps." He led them with distinction in the Antietam campaign, at Fredericksburg in December, and at Chancellorsville in May 1863, where he proved himself to be iron-willed and always cool in action.

Given command of a division in III Corps, Humphreys held off attacks at Gettysburg (1–3 July 1863) by superior Confederate forces. For this action he was named a major-general of volunteers, as well as a brevet brigadier-general in the regular army. General Meade asked him to become chief of staff of the Army of the Potomac, in which appointment he served until November 1864. The initial announcement came as a surprise to many; Marsena Patrick noted in his diary on 9 July, "Gen. Humphreys was announced as Chief of Staff, to the surprise of all, as it has been understood that Gen. Warren would have that position." Patrick did not think much of Humphreys' suitability; however, his service met with the approval of Meade and, later, of Grant.

When Winfield Hancock's ill health forced him to give up his command in November 1864, Grant picked Humphreys to take over the veteran but worn-down II Corps. Grant's aide, Horace Porter, reflected headquarters thinking when he wrote, "His appointment was recognized as eminently fitting, and met with favor throughout the entire army"; but this was not wholly true. John Gibbon, the senior divisional commander in the corps, took great exception to being passed over. He asked to be relieved, while assuring Humphreys that he was doing so not out of a refusal to serve under him but because he felt he was being slighted. As to Humphreys, Gibbon said, the general was "one of the most accomplished soldiers and highest-toned gentlemen in the army." Luckily for the army, Grant declined to give in to Gibbon, whom he retained in command of his division.

Humphreys did an excellent job in revitalizing the II Corps, leading it in all operations up to Appomattox. He was given the rank of brevet major-general in the regular army for his gallantry at Sailor's Creek. After the war, in August 1866 he was named a brigadier-general in the regular army, with the post of chief of engineers. He served in this position until he retired in 1879. He also produced an excellent account entitled *The Virginia Campaign of 1864–65*. He died in Washington, DC on 27 December 1883.

HUNT, Henry Jackson (1819–89)

Henry Hunt (**see Plate C3**) was born in Detroit on 14 September 1819. A third-generation regular army officer, Hunt was graduated from West Point in 1839. He served as a lieutenant of artillery in Winfield Scott's audacious advance on Mexico City in August 1847, earning brevets to captain and major for gallantry. At Churubusco he galloped his gun up to the walls of the capital; as the gun unlimbered almost every man and horse was hit, but the survivors got the piece into position only yards from a Mexican gun. Both crews were loading with desperate haste, but in the end it was Hunt's gun that fired first. After the Mexican War, Hunt was named to a board of three artillerymen who were to revise the system of light artillery tactics then in use. Their manual was adopted by the army in 1860 and became the standard system for both sides in the Civil War.

Hunt served at First Bull Run (Manassas – 21 July 1861) and was then named chief of artillery for the Washington defenses; he was also given responsibility for training the artillery reserve of the Army of the Potomac. Hunt pioneered massed artillery use in the Union army, assembling at Malvern Hill (1 July 1862) some 100 guns, which almost alone broke up the Confederate attacks. He served with distinction at Antietam (17 September 1862), being named a brigadier-general of volunteers two days before the battle.

Although a regular army man, and known for dressing down battery commanders for wasting expensive ammunition, Hunt was informal with his staff. Provost Marshal Marsena Patrick, himself somewhat stiff-necked, noted in his diary on 31 December 1862 – New Year's Eve – that he went to bed at a quarter of ten, "but was again roused by the Card players at Hunt['s] Tent – I remained awake an hour, then wrote a note & sent it, a little after 12 o'clock, requesting the noise to be stopped."

At Gettysburg (1–3 July 1863) Hunt placed 77 guns along the Union front, withdrawing several batteries there during the counter-battery fight with the Confederate guns given the job of softening up the Union center for Pickett's Charge. He got them back, with enough ammunition for the job, in time to help stop the attack; and was breveted major-general of volunteers for his service. However, Hunt, a Democrat, stayed in contact with George McClellan, who ran for president against Lincoln; and in September 1864 Hunt wrote to McClellan that an armistice with the South could lead to peace, and the Democratic Party platform was aimed at the South "to detach the people from their leaders," and should be supported by McClellan.

In June 1864, Ulysses S.Grant placed Hunt in charge of all siege operations at Petersburg. At the end of the war he was named a major-general in the regular army, but reverted to his permanent rank of

Henry Hunt, the brilliant and highly successful Army of the Potomac artillery commander, with Maj. James Duane, the army's chief engineer, in the lines at Petersburg, as shown in an engraving in the 15 October 1864 issue of *Harper's Weekly*. In March 1865 a subordinate, Col. Charles Wainwright, recalled a ride along Union lines in Hunt's company: "The General was in the most excellent spirits, and amused me very much as well as filling me with wonder at his memory... quoting page after page; and then almost whole volumes of comic poetry, interspersed with stories. Still he saw everything as we rode along and was just as much alive to the object of his visit to the lines as if he had been thinking and talking of nothing else. He is certainly one of the most wonderful men I have ever met. With a very retentive memory, he is always forgetting; most original and practical in all his ideas, he is most impractical in carrying them out... ." Nevertheless, Hunt had shown heroism and energy as a young officer of the "flying artillery" in the Mexican War.

lieutenant-colonel in the 3rd US Artillery. He was named colonel commanding the 5th US Artillery in 1869, serving until he retired in 1883. He was appointed governor of the Soldiers' Home in Washington in 1885, dying there on 11 February 1889.

KEARNY, Philip (1815–62)

Philip Kearny was born in New York City on 2 June 1815. The scion of a wealthy, socially prominent family, he was graduated from Columbia University in 1833. He inherited a million dollars in 1836 – an almost unimaginable sum at that date – but nevertheless decided to follow his dream into the army. Commissioned into his uncle's regiment, the 1st Dragoons, in 1837 as a second lieutenant, Kearny attended the French cavalry school at Saumur in 1839. He served with the Chasseurs d'Afrique in Algiers in 1840, returning to serve on the staff of the Major-General Commanding the Army.

On Winfield Scott's staff in Mexico, at Churubusco (20 August 1847) Kearny was badly wounded in the left arm, which was subsequently amputated. Recovering, he then served in California until he resigned in 1851. He then traveled the world before retiring to his New Jersey estate. In 1859 he went to Europe to join the French Imperial Guard in the Italian campaign of that year, serving at Solferino and Magenta.

On the outbreak of the Civil War, Kearny returned to the army and was quickly appointed a brigadier-general of volunteers in command of a New Jersey brigade. He was made a major-general on 4 July 1862, commanding a division in III Corps in the Peninsula campaign. Proud of his own men, he once addressed some stragglers only to find that they were from a different command. To ensure that this never happened again, on 27 June 1862 he issued the following order: "The general commanding division directs that officers in command of companies are to wear a piece of red flannel two inches square on the front of their caps. Field officers to wear the same upon the top of the cap – this to be done immediately that they may be recognized in action." After Kearny's death the practice was ordered continued, and enlisted men also began wearing these "Kearny's patches". This was the origin of what would become an army-wide system of divisional identification after Hooker took over.

The extraordinary Philip Kearny – an engraving in *Harper's Weekly* of 20 September 1862, after a Brady photograph. According to the paper, "General McClellan is said to have wept when he heard of his death, and to have said: 'Who can replace Phil Kearney?' ". The inheritor of enormous wealth, this hero of the battle of Churubusco (1847) still pursued the profession of arms so hungrily that when US Army service palled he traveled to serve with the French army in North Africa and Italy. Note that the engraving process has reversed the portrait left for right – it was Kearny's left arm that he lost in Mexico, and his coat is shown here buttoning the female way.

Kearny was unhappy with what he perceived as timidity among the Union senior commanders. After the Peninsula campaign had stalled Charles Wainwright confided to his diary, "[Kearny] is full of the possibility of our capturing Richmond at this time; says he could do it with his division, and that two or three divisions could do it easily. He talked very wild, as usual. Still, there may be something in what he says."

Kearny would never have the chance to be tested at any higher level of command than a division. At Chantilly, on 1 September 1862, in a heavy rain storm, he rode by accident into Confederate lines. Called on to surrender, he spurred his horse instead and, while trying to escape, was shot and killed. Lee himself sent a message through the lines reporting Kearny's death, and his body was turned over to Union authorities to be returned to his family. He was originally buried at Trinity Church, New York City, but in 1912 was reburied in Arlington National Cemetery.

Colonel David Strother noted in his diary on 2 September 1862: "Heard the news that General Kearny had been killed last night and his body sent in by the enemy under a flag. Thus ends the one-armed hero of the war, a man of great valor and energy and a serious loss for us." This was the general opinion of the army.

McCLELLAN, George Brinton (1826–85)

George McClellan (**see Plate C1**) was born in Philadelphia on 3 December 1826. Attending the University of Pennsylvania, he left in order to enter West Point, where he was graduated second in his class of

1846. Appointed to the Corps of Engineers, he was noted for getting roads and bridges built during Scott's Mexico City campaign of 1847, earning two brevets. Thereafter he returned to West Point as an instructor; translated a French bayonet manual; explored the sources of the Red River; was one of a group of US Army observers during the Crimean War; designed a saddle for army use that was based on the Hungarian model; and surveyed possible transcontinental railroad routes. He resigned his commission as captain, 1st Cavalry, in 1857 to become chief engineer of the Illinois Central Railroad.

At the outbreak of the Civil War he was president of the Ohio & Mississippi Railroad; he volunteered his services to Ohio's governor, who on 23 April 1861 appointed McClellan a major-general to organize the state forces. So well did he perform this task that President Lincoln appointed him a major-general in the regular army – as its second ranking officer – in June 1861.

McClellan was successful in West Virginia in June and July – a time of few successes – and Lincoln brought him East to command the Army of the Potomac in August, naming him General-in-Chief of the Armies of the United States on 1 November 1861 in succession to Winfield Scott. He set about rebuilding the army's morale, getting clothes and food for the troops, while holding parade after parade to instil pride and confidence. McClellan himself did not lack for confidence, writing on 21 May 1862, "When I see the hand of God guarding one so weak as myself, I can almost think myself a chosen instrument to carry out his schemes."

In March 1862, President Lincoln, frustrated by McClellan's inactivity, relieved him of his generalship-in-chief to concentrate on his army command and gave him a direct order to take the field. McClellan finally shipped his Army of the Potomac to the Peninsula that juts into Chesapeake Bay, planning a rapid march to take Richmond. Faulty intelligence, which he believed despite evidence to the contrary, indicated that Confederate forces greatly out-numbered him. After making laborious preparations to conduct a siege at Yorktown that never happened, the Union army almost reached Richmond, only to be attacked by the Confederates under Joseph Johnston (Fair Oaks, 31 May–1 June), and then again under Robert E.Lee (Gaine's Mill, 27 June). McClellan, thoroughly unnerved by these attacks, rejected the advice of Kearny and Hooker that Richmond was still vulnerable, and withdrew to a defendable base on the James River.

He was then ordered to bring the army back to northern Virginia to support John Pope's abortive campaign, which failed at

Blessed with a versatile mind and sweeping interests, George McClellan made a technically perfect commander for the Army of the Potomac, in which appointment his handsome looks and gentlemanly manners also earned him many admirers. However, his unshakable self-confidence was allied to excessive caution, and a total lack of political instinct; and when his lack of nerve in combat situations led to repeated failure in 1862, Lincoln dismissed him. That this came as a complete surprise to him says much about McClellan's limitations.

Second Bull Run (Manassas – 30 August). As Lee headed into Maryland, McClellan followed, and even had the luck to obtain a copy of Lee's battle plan. Moving rapidly – for McClellan – he struck Lee's divided army at Antietam (17 September). The Union attacks were piecemeal, however, and Lee's greatly outnumbered forces held, inflicting great losses; two days later they withdrew across the Potomac, unmolested.

McClellan followed Lee with characteristic caution. Lincoln visited his headquarters; but unable to persuade him to act aggressively, the President dismissed McClellan from command of the Army of the Potomac and replaced him with Ambrose Burnside on 7 November 1862. Most of the army were as shocked as was McClellan. "The greatest indignation is expressed by everyone here, even those who have blamed McClellan [for the army's failure to succeed]," Charles Wainwright wrote in his dairy the next day. On the 9th he noted that some officers, on McClellan's farewell, used "expressions with regret to his removal which they had no right to use, and a few even going so far as to beg him to resist the order, and saying that the army would support him." Even a private in the 9th New York, Edward Wightman, wrote home that "there seems to be a general impression that this is no time to change field officers… ."

McClellan went home to Trenton, New Jersey, fully expecting orders to resume his command; but they never came. The Democratic Party nominated this conservative to run against Lincoln in the 1864 presidential election on a peace platform. He duly resigned his commission on election day; but his bid failed, in part due to Lincoln's overwhelming support from soldiers who voted in the field. McClellan later became governor of New Jersey; he died on 19 October 1885 at Orange, New Jersey, and was buried in Riverview Cemetery, Trenton.

In 1866 William Swinton, who had been a reporter for the *New York Times* during the war, wrote a history of the army, which he had accompanied. Of McClellan he wrote: "He was assuredly not a great general; for he had the pedantry of war rather than the inspiration of war. His talent was eminently that of the cabinet; and his proper place was in Washington, where he should have remained as general-in-chief. Here his ability to plan campaigns and form large strategic combinations, which was remarkable, would have had full scope; and he would have been considerate and helpful to those in the field. But his power as a tactician was much inferior to his talent as a strategist, and he executed less boldly than he conceived: not appearing to know well those counters with which a commander must work – time, place, and circumstance."

McClellan was unusual among general officers in nearly always being photographed wearing his buff sash; he was also known for being accompanied by a large staff when in the field. This photograph was taken in the fall of 1861.

McDOWELL, Irvin (1818–85)

Irvin McDowell (**see Plate A3**) was born in Columbus, Ohio, on 15 October 1818. At first educated in France, he was graduated in the US

Military Academy class of 1838, and taught tactics at the Academy from 1841 to 1845. He served as a staff officer in the Mexican War, earning a captain's brevet for gallantry at Buena Vista (22 February 1847). From then until the outbreak of the Civil War he was assigned to duty in the office of the Adjutant General of the Army.

On 14 May 1861 he was appointed a brigadier-general in the regular army, although he had exercised no command until that point. He was given command of the Army of the Potomac and directed to lead it on Richmond. McDowell believed that the army was unready to take the field, and later testified to Congress: "There was not a man there who had ever manoeuvred troops in large bodies. There was not one in the army; I did not believe there was one in the whole country; at least, I knew there was no one there who had ever handled 30,000 troops. I had seen them handled abroad in reviews and marched, but I have never handled that number, and no one here had. I wanted very much a little time; all of us wanted it. We did not have a bit of it. The answer was: 'You are green, it is true; but they are green, also; you are all green alike'."

His campaign plan was a good one, but his ill-trained force fell apart at First Bull Run (Manassas) on 21 July, and he was replaced in command of the army by George McClellan. In March 1862 he was named a major-general of volunteers and given command of a corps in the Army of the Potomac. His corps was left to defend Washington during the Peninsula campaign, but took the field in the Second Bull Run campaign in summer 1862.

Colonel David Strother met McDowell in June 1862 and noted in his diary: "His manner is not strong but his conversation was clear and concise, showing a good understanding of the subject in hand." A month later he had a chance to talk further with McDowell: "Sitting down, we had a very pleasant half of an hour [talking] chiefly about trouting, of which he is very fond. His manners are very kind and he talks agreeably… ."

McDowell was blamed for the army's defeat in the Second Bull Run campaign almost as much as was John Pope, its commander. It had not helped him that many of his troops, at all levels, basically distrusted his loyalty to the Union. McDowell himself complained to Marsena Patrick on 12 July 1862 "that [Brig.Gen. Abner] Doubleday has been the cause of more evil to him than any one else, having made the matter of his guarding rebel property the test of his loyalty".

McDowell was relieved from command and spent two years of inactivity, finally being assigned as commander of the Department of the Pacific on 1 July 1864. He later commanded both the Department of the East and that of the South before returning to command the Department of the Pacific. He died in San Francisco on 4 May 1885, and is buried at the Presidio there.

Irvin McDowell had the ill fortune to be the first commander of the wholly unprepared Army of the Potomac in its unsuccessful First Bull Run (Manassas) campaign of July 1861. He had previously been involved with construction projects in Washington, DC, as a professional engineer, and as a long-time staff officer he had very little experience of command. He was perfectly well aware of his own and his army's failings, but was unjustly blamed for the outcome when the government forced him into premature action.

MEADE, George Gordon (1815–72)

George Meade (see Plate E1) was born in Cadiz, Spain, on 31 December 1815, the son of a wealthy American merchant who was wiped out financially by adhering to Spain's cause in the Napoleonic Wars. Returning to the United States, Meade attended Mount Hope Institution and then the US Military Academy, from which he was graduated in 1835. He saw service in Florida and at the Watertown Arsenal before resigning in 1836 to work as a civil engineer. He returned to the army on 19 May 1842 as a second lieutenant in the Corps of Topographical Engineers, thereafter working mostly on building lighthouses and breakwaters and doing coastal and geodetic survey work. He saw action in the Mexican War, being breveted a first lieutenant.

At the outbreak of the Civil War, Capt. Meade was made a brigadier-general of volunteers and given command of a Pennsylvania brigade, which he led in the Peninsula campaign. He was badly wounded at Glendale (30 June 1862), one of the defensive battles fought by dispersed Union corps as they retreated to the James River. Recovering in time for Second Bull Run (Manassas), he was given command of a division in I Corps at Fredericksburg (13 December 1862); shortly thereafter he was given V Corps. He was named to replace Joseph Hooker as commander of the Army of the Potomac on 28 June 1863, just three days before Gettysburg. The army's fifth commander in just ten months, his personal contribution to the Union's great victory in that battle has always been a matter for discussion, and he was criticized for failing to pursue the retreating Confederates vigorously. Marsena Patrick noted in his diary on 16 November 1863 that Meade was "profoundly ignorant of the wants & necessities of the Army," adding that he would probably "never learn."

Staff officer Frank Haskell described Meade as "a tall spare man, with full beard, which with his hair, originally brown, is quite thickly sprinkled with gray – has a romanish face, very large nose, and a white, large forehead, prominent and wide over the eyes, which are full and large, and quick in their movements, and he wears spectacles. His *fibres* are all of the long and sinewy kind. His habitual personal appearance is quite careless, and it would be difficult to make him look well dressed."

Meade was terribly short-tempered. While leading a column of prisoners to the rear during the fighting in the Wilderness, Patrick noted in his diary that he "met Meade, who was in a terrible stew & declared that I was on the wrong road & going directly into the enemy's lines – I soon cooled him off however & in a huff was told to 'Go my own way', which I did, keeping the prisoners on the road they started, all right."

Although Lincoln was unhappy that Lee was allowed to escape from Gettysburg, Meade retained his army command right through to Appomattox. He was named a brigadier-general

George Gordon Meade as a major-general. Meade thought that he would be replaced as commander of the Army of the Potomac after earning Lincoln's displeasure for his failure to destroy Lee's army after Gettysburg, at Bristoe Station, and at Mine Run; but he was retained in command until the end of the war. He looks lugubrious in portraits, but was known for his hot temper: a contemporary called him a "damned old goggle eyed snapping turtle."

George Meade, standing center right foreground, facing left; the general in the bowler-type hat and open-necked coat standing behind Meade at right is John Sedgwick. They are seen here with their staffs at their head-quarters in Falmouth, Virginia, in late 1863.

in the regular army on 7 July 1863, and a major-general late in the war. He held commands of various departments after the war, eventually being in charge of the Division of the Atlantic. He died at his headquarters in Philadelphia on 6 November 1872, and is buried in Laurel Hill Cemetery there. After the war, Grant wrote:

"General Meade was an officer of great merit, with drawbacks to his usefulness that were beyond his control. He had been an officer of the engineer corps before the war, and consequently had never served with troops until he was over forty-six years of age. He never had, I believe, a command of less than a brigade. He saw clearly and distinctly the position of the enemy, and the topography of the country in front of his own position. His first idea was to take advantage of the lay of the ground, sometimes without reference to the direction we wanted to move afterwards. He was subordinate to his superiors in rank to the extent that he could execute an order which changed his own plans with the same zeal he would have displayed if the plan had been his own. He was brave and conscientious, and commanded the respect of all who knew him. He was unfortunately of a temper that would get beyond his control, at times, and make him speak to officers of high rank in the most offensive manner. No one saw this fault more plainly than he himself, and no one regretted it more. This made it unpleasant at times, even in battle, for those around him to approach him even with information."

(continued on page 43)

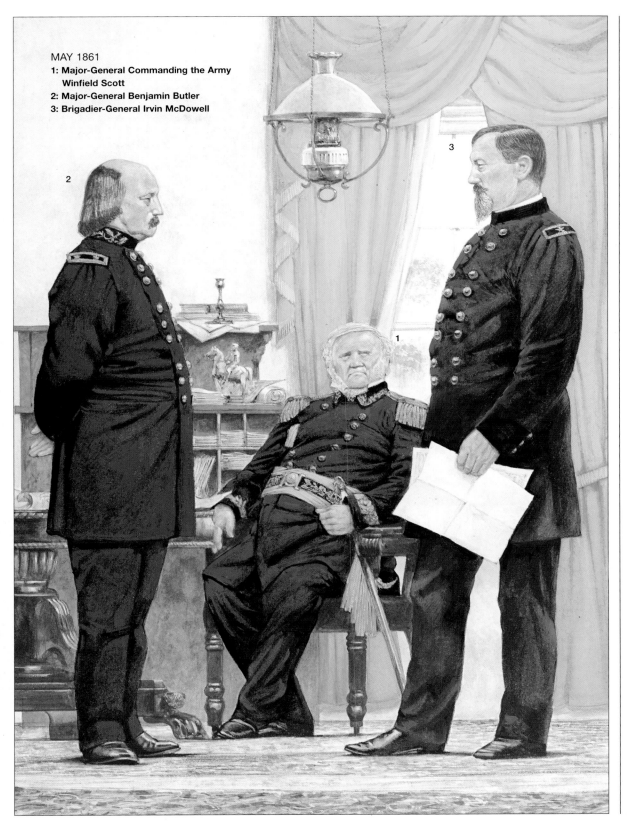

MAY 1861
1: Major-General Commanding the Army
   Winfield Scott
2: Major-General Benjamin Butler
3: Brigadier-General Irvin McDowell

A

AUGUST 1862
1: Major-General John Pope
2: Major-General Fitz John Porter
3: Major-General Edwin Sumner

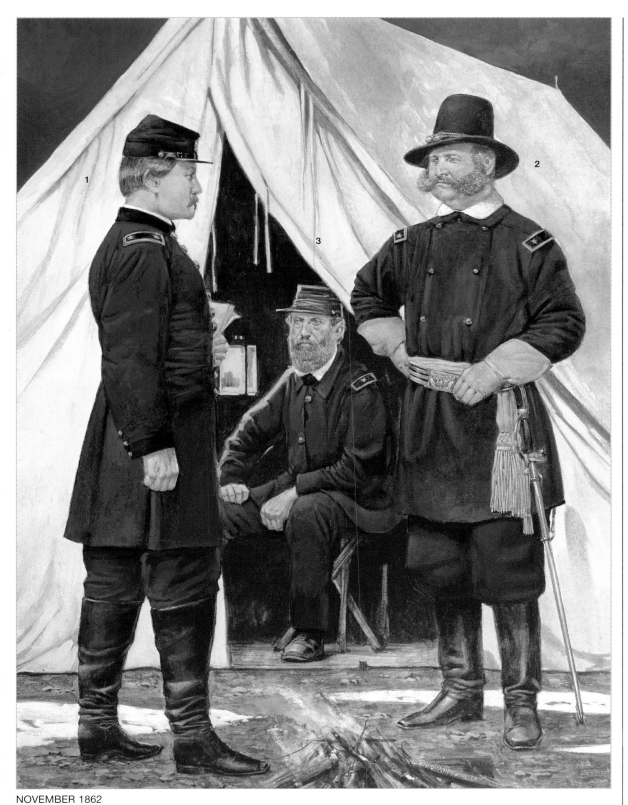

NOVEMBER 1862
1: Major-General George McClellan   2: Major-General Ambrose Burnside   3: Brigadier-General Henry Hunt

C

MAY 1863
1: Major-General Joseph Hooker 2: Major-General Darius Couch 3: Major-General William Franklin

D

JUNE 1863
1: Major-General George Meade
2: Major-General John Reynolds
3: Major-General Daniel Sickles

E

II CORPS COMMANDERS, AUTUMN 1864
1: Major-General Winfield Scott Hancock
2: Brigadier-General Francis Barlow
3: Brigadier-General John Gibbon

F

CAVALRY COMMANDERS OF THE ARMY OF THE POTOMAC
1: Brigadier-General George Stoneman   2: Major-General Alfred Pleasonton   3: Major-General Philip Sheridan

PETERSBURG, MAY 1864
1: Major-General Andrew Humphreys
2: Major-General John Sedgwick
3: Major-General Joshua Chamberlain

H

PLEASONTON, Alfred (1824–97)

Alfred Pleasonton (**see Plate G2**) was born in Washington, DC on 7 July 1824. Graduated in the West Point class of 1844, he was assigned to the dragoons. He earned a first lieutenant's brevet for gallantry in the Mexican War, and also served in Florida and on the frontier. He gained staff experience as an adjutant under Gen. William S.Harney. In 1861 he was a captain in the 2nd Dragoons (redesignated the 2nd Cavalry), and commanded the regiment as it marched from Utah to Washington that fall.

Promoted major on 15 February 1862, Pleasonton distinguished himself in the Peninsula campaign, and was made a brigadier-general of volunteers on 18 July 1862. He was given command of a cavalry division in the Antietam campaign, leading it at Fredericksburg (13 December 1862) and Chancellorsville (1–6 May 1863). He was given command of the Cavalry Corps of the Army of the Potomac on 7 June 1863, with promotion to major-general on 22 June.

Pleasonton was regarded with some suspicion by his peers. Colonel Charles R.Lowell, 2nd Massachusetts, said of him: "I can't call any cavalry officer good who can't see the truth and tell the truth. With an infantry officer this is not so essential, but cavalry are the eyes and ears of the army and ought to see and hear and tell truly; and yet it is the universal opinion that P's own reputation and P's late promotions are bolstered up by systematic lying." Captain Charles Francis Adams Jr, 1st Massachusetts, wrote to his mother that "Pleasonton is the bete noire of all cavalry officers… He is pure and simple a newspaper humbug. You always see his name in the papers, but to us who have served under him he is notorious as a bully and a toady… Yet mean and contemptible as Pleasonton is, he is always *in* at Head Quarters."

Brig.Gen. Alfred Pleasonton wears a typical field uniform of a sack coat and a broad-brimmed hat in this photograph taken in April 1863.

However, Pleasonton was well respected by at least some of the army's commanders. In a letter to his wife on 18 August 1862, McClellan said: "I am glad to inform you that your friend Pleasonton has done *splendidly*. I placed him in command of the rear guard. The little fellow [Pleasonton] brightened up very much this morning when he came to report. I looked very sternly at him & told him that I had a very serious complaint to make against him. He looked rather wild, injured, & disgusted & wished to know what it was. I replied that he had entirely disappointed me, that he had not created a single stampede, nor called for any reinforcements. That such heinous conduct was something I did not at all look for, & that if it was persisted in, I must send him to Pope. The little fellow began to grin & was well pleased. He *is* a most excellent soldier & has performed a very important duty most admirably."

Pleasonton led the cavalry in its first successful large operation of the war, surprising J.E.B.Stuart at Brandy Station (9 June 1863), in which action the Union cavalry was said to have come of age. However, his work in the Gettysburg campaign

was lackluster. He disapproved of the "Kilpatrick-Dahlgren Raid" against Richmond in February 1864, something that Grant thought was a good idea. As Grant had in mind for Philip Sheridan to command the cavalry in the East, this disagreement was the spur for Pleasonton's relief from command and reassignment to the Department of the Missouri.

There he performed well enough against the Confederate "Missouri Raid" in October 1864. Breveted major-general at the end of the war, he still reverted to his regular rank of major, 2nd US Cavalry. In 1866 Pleasonton was offered a lieutenant-colonelcy in the 20th US Infantry, but declined it. Since this resulted in his being subordinate to Col. T.J.H.Wood, who had graduated from West Point a year after Pleasonton and was lower on the list of volunteer major-generals, and to Lt.Col. I.N.Palmer, who graduated two years after Pleasonton and had only been breveted major-general, Pleasonton resigned. Although he applied for retirement at his volunteer rank, this was refused. He held some minor Federal posts, but in 1888 he was placed on the retired list as a major. He died in Washington on 17 February 1897, and is buried in the Congressional Cemetery there.

POPE, John (1822–92)

John Pope (**see Plate B1**) was born into a distinguished family in Louisville, Kentucky, on 16 March 1822. After graduating from West Point in 1842, he was twice breveted in the Mexican War. Commissioned a captain in the Corps of Topographical Engineers in 1856, he was named a brigadier-general of volunteers on 14 June 1861.

Pope led the forces that opened the upper Mississippi River just above Memphis, capturing Madrid and Island No.10. Promoted to major-general on 22 March 1862, he commanded the left wing of the army that besieged Corinth, Mississippi. Because of these successes he was called to Washington to command a new Army of Virginia, made up of troops around Washington and in the Shenandoah Valley.

Colonel David Strother met Pope in June 1862, and described him in his diary: "He is a stout man of medium height, prepossessing manners and appearance. He is young and alert… ." Later he added: "He reads character and talks like a keen, cool man of the world, kindly withal… Pope is a much cleverer man than I took him for." Two months later Strother wrote: "Pope is a bright, dashing man, self-confident and clearheaded. He has a good memory and has been a topographical engineer. I observe that he is wonderfully quick to seize all information on this subject. He remembers it all if once told and wants new details. Whether his mind grasps general subjects with capacity and clearness I have not had an opportunity to judge. He is irascible and impulsive in his judgments of men, but in his pleasant moods, jolly, humorous, and clever in conversation."

Named a brigadier-general in the regular army with effect from 14 July 1862, Pope issued a series of orders, the first telling his new command, "I have come to you from the West, where we have always seen the backs of our enemies… ." Having irritated his own troops, he made the enemy even madder by calling for his troops to live off the resources of Virginia's citizens, and authorizing them to inflict capital punishment on any guerrillas who had sworn an oath of allegiance to the USA and were later captured in arms against the government. Lee determined to decisively beat Pope's army, which he did in the Second Bull Run (Manassas) campaign of August 1862. Many of Pope's own generals were highly critical of him, both before and after Second Manassas.

Pope's army was afterwards merged into the Army of the Potomac, and he was sent to command the Department of the Northwest. He served well there during the Sioux uprising in Minnesota in 1863. Staying in the army after the war, he became a major-general on 26 October 1882 and held various departmental commands until his retirement in 1886. He died in Sandusky,

Fitz John Porter was tall, striking, a perfect-looking soldier, but lacked the political instincts needed to survive. He foolishly committed to paper criticisms of his superior officer, John Pope, which would come back to haunt him.

Ohio, on 23 September 1892, and is buried in Bellefontaine Cemetery, St Louis.

PORTER, Fitz John (1822–1901)

Fitz John Porter (**see Plate B2**) was born in Portsmouth, New Hampshire, to a naval family that included Commodore David Porter and Rear Admiral David Dixon Porter. He attended Exeter and was appointed to West Point, graduating in 1845. He was assigned to the artillery, and during the Mexican War he was wounded in the attack on Mexico City and received two brevets for gallantry. After the war he was assigned as an assistant artillery instructor at West Point until 1855. He was then adjutant of the command sent to Utah in 1857, serving there until 1860.

At the outbreak of the Civil War he was made colonel of the 15th US Infantry, as well as a brigadier-general of volunteers ranking from 17 May 1861. He served as chief of staff under Gen. Robert Patterson in the Shenandoah Valley during the First Bull Run campaign, before being recalled to help George McClellan whip the new Army of the Potomac into shape.

Porter commanded a division of III Corps at the outset of the Peninsula campaign, moving up to command of V Corps during the Seven Days' Battles. He displayed outstanding leadership in extricating his corps from constant attacks by superior Confederate forces, withdrawing to Malvern Hill, where he oversaw a huge defeat of the attacking Confederates (1 July 1862). For this action he was promoted to major-general of volunteers, as well as receiving a brevet to brigadier-general in the regular army.

When McClellan's army was withdrawn from the Peninsula to aid Pope's army in northern Virginia, Porter was ordered to come to Pope's aid; but *New York Times* reporter William Swinton, who covered the Army of the Potomac, wrote that "the order which Pope sent at half-past four, did not reach Porter till about dusk. He then made dispositions for attack, but it was too late. It is, however, more than doubtful that even had the order been received in time, any thing but repulse would have resulted from its execution."

Afterwards, Porter, who despised Pope, was discovered to have written about the latter in insubordinate terms. Knowing how close Porter was to McClellan, Pope, unable to have McClellan himself court-martialed, instead charged Porter with disloyalty, disobedience and misconduct in the face of the enemy. Porter, who advised McClellan not to commit his V Corps to a final attack at Antietam (17 September 1862), and hence allowed Lee to escape total defeat, was relieved from command after McClellan's own relief left him unprotected. He was tried by a military commission. Charles Wainwright, a McClellan supporter who suspected that the actual reason was the friendship between McClellan and Porter, added: "On the whole I cannot say that I am sorry, for I think I shall like Reynolds quite as much, and have a great deal more respect from him."

The commission found Porter guilty, and on 21 January 1863 ordered him "forever disqualified from holding any office of trust or profit under the Government of the United States." Wainwright felt that "From the manner of getting up the charges and of the formation of the court, I made up my mind at once that the case was to go against him. It was necessary for the Administration that it should: some scapegoat had to be found for the shortcomings of their pet, Pope, and in Porter they could hit a friend of McClellan at the same time. He may have been guilty of everything charged against him, or he may have been perfectly innocent, of this I know nothing; his condemnation was a foregone conclusion."

Porter spent the next 16 years seeking reinstatement to the US Army. Finally, a board headed by Gen. John M.Schofield exonerated Porter on 19 March 1879, and recommended his reinstatement. The current president, Republican Rutherford B.Hayes – who had actually lost the election but obtained office through political maneuvering – declined to act on the board's findings. Finally, on 4 May 1882, President Chester Arthur – a Democrat on the opposite side of the political fence from Hayes – ordered a full remission of the findings of the Porter court-martial, restoring his rank as a colonel of infantry from 14 May 1861. Porter died in Morristown, New Jersey, on 21 May 1901, and was buried in Green-Wood Cemetery, Brooklyn, New York.

Porter (seated, center) and his staff at his headquarters, photographed not long after the battle of Gaines' Mill (27 June 1862), where Porter had managed to extract his corps from heavy Confederate assaults. A close associate of McClellan, Porter fell when McClellan fell, but in fact his bad advice at Antietam essentially ensured that Lee would manage to save his army from destruction.

REYNOLDS, John Fulton (1820–63)

John Reynolds (**see Plate E2**) was born in Lancaster, Pennsylvania, on 20 September 1820. After attending Lancaster County Academy he was graduated from West Point in 1841. He served as an artillery officer on the Atlantic coast and in Texas before the Mexican War, in which he was breveted a captain and major for gallant and meritorious conduct. After years of garrison duty, he became Commandant of Cadets at West Point in September 1860, leaving the Academy to become lieutenant-colonel of the 14th US Infantry on 14 May 1861, and a brigadier-general of volunteers on 26 August.

Reynolds commanded the 1st Brigade of Pennsylvania Reserves, raised from excess volunteers from that state, which was assigned to the Army of the Potomac. The men of his brigade had a chance to appreciate Reynolds' coolness in the field during their first experience at the front. Major Evan Woodward, 2nd Reserves, recalled in his history of the Reserves published in 1865: "When we first commenced our retrograde movement many surmises that soon assumed the shape of rumors were set afloat, and as we at that time were incapable of judging of military

movements, they received much credence. An orderly came dashing down the road in search of General Reynolds and almost breathlessly informed him, there were 'forty thousand rebels coming down upon us'. 'Forty thousand old fools', replied the General, 'go back to where you came from'."

Reynolds' brigade was assigned to V Corps in the Peninsula campaign where he, along with his adjutant, was surprised and captured on the night of 27 June 1862. Exchanged on 8 August, he was given command of the 3rd Division of Pennsylvania Reserves in the Second Bull Run (Manassas) campaign. During the Antietam campaign he commanded Pennsylvania militia, and he received command of I Corps of the Army of the Potomac before Fredericksburg (December 1862), at which battle he distinguished himself by his energy and courage.

On 29 November 1862 he was named a major-general of volunteers. Declining to accept command of the Army of the Potomac to replace Hooker, he was appointed by the army's new commander, George Meade, to command the first three corps on the field at Gettysburg. Charles Wainwright noted in his diary: "General Reynolds told me today that the command of this army was offered to him when he was summoned up to Washington a month ago; but he refused it, because, to use his own expression, 'he was unwilling to take Burnside and Hooker's leavings'."

While bringing up the 2nd Wisconsin Infantry to help hold the line at Gettysburg, Reynolds was shot and killed instantly by a Confederate infantryman in a barn on the edge of nearby woodland. He was buried in the main burial plot at Lancaster, only 50 miles away from Gettysburg. He had fallen without receiving a presentation sword, with a blade of the finest Damascus steel, a black onyx grip set with the initials "J.F.R." in diamonds, and a scabbard of pure gold, which had been acquired earlier without a chance for a formal presentation ceremony. The scabbard was engraved, "Presented to Major-general John F. Reynolds, by the enlisted men of the First, Second, Fifth and Eighth regiments of the First Brigade of Pennsylvania, in testimony of their love and admiration. Mechanicsville, June 26th, 1862." The sword was finally presented to Reynolds' sister.

RICKETTS, James Brewerton (1817–87)

James Ricketts was a native of New York City, born on 21 June 1817 into an old family which had settled in New Jersey in the early colonial period. In 1835 he was appointed to West Point, graduating in 1839. Ricketts was commissioned a second lieutenant in the 1st US Artillery and sent to the Canadian frontier. In 1840 he married Harriet Josephine Pierce, who died young, leaving the widowed lieutenant to care for a child. In the Mexican War his artillery battery was assigned to the army under Maj.Gen. Zachary Taylor, fighting at Monterey (20–24 September 1846) and Buena Vista (22–23 February 1847). After the war he was sent to Florida, where he was promoted captain on 3 August 1852. He married Francis Lawrence in 1856; they eventually had five children, of whom only two would grow to adulthood.

The outbreak of the Civil War would find Ricketts as senior captain in the 1st Artillery in command of Company I, which was overrun at First Bull Run (Manassas) on 21 July 1861; badly wounded in the leg, he was taken prisoner. He was exchanged on 20 December and, after leave to

James Ricketts, who as an artillery lieutenant in the 1840s had been left a widower with a small child. He remarried in 1856, and the second Mrs Ricketts – no beauty, and taller than her husband – seems to have taken to army life admirably. The diarist Marsena Patrick, who had known Ricketts from 1835 when they were both at West Point, recorded meeting her in camp in October 1862: "Mrs R. read to me her report of the 2nd Bull Run. She came on here to write it for her husband. She says that from the time she was married, she has always made out his Muster Rolls & Reports... ."

recuperate, on 30 April 1862 he returned to duty and was assigned to command a brigade in the Army of the Rappahannock, being commissioned a brigadier-general of volunteers to rank from 21 July 1862.

On 10 June, Ricketts was named to command the 2nd Division in III Corps, and fought at Cedar Mountain (9 August), Second Bull Run (Manassas – 29–30 August), and Antietam (17 September) – there is some disagreement as to whether or not he was wounded there. At any rate, he left his command on 4 October 1862 and went to Washington, where he served on various commissions and courts-martial until 4 April 1864.

Ricketts was then given command of the 3rd Division, VI Corps; he was offered corps command on John Sedgwick's death but he turned it down, saying that Sedgwick had wanted one of the other divisional commanders to succeed him. The corps was sent to help defend Washington during "Early's Raid", and Ricketts' division fought on the Monocacy River. For his part in the battle, on 1 August 1864 he was commissioned a major-general of volunteers. VI Corps went on to serve in Philip Sheridan's Valley campaign thereafter, and Ricketts was commanding it at Cedar Creek (19 October 1864) when he was badly wounded in the chest and right shoulder. He returned to duty on 7 April 1865, just two days before Lee's surrender at Appomattox.

After the war Ricketts reverted to the rank of major, retiring in January 1867. However, he was so much admired that he continued to serve on courts-martial until 1869. Suffering greatly from the effects of his old wounds, he died on 22 September 1887, and was buried in Arlington National Cemetery.

SCOTT, Winfield (1786–1866)

Winfield Scott (see Plate A1) was quite possibly the greatest soldier the United States ever produced; he had the bad luck, however, to fight in the country's minor wars rather than her major ones. He was born near Petersburg, Virginia, on 13 June 1786, but was orphaned at an early age. He was graduated from William and Mary in 1804 and then studied law. However, rather than practice, he accepted an artillery captain's commission in 1808. He became a lieutenant-colonel in 1812 and adjutant general, ranking as a colonel, in March 1813.

During the War of 1812 he was captured by the British at Queenstown Heights but soon exchanged. Colonel Scott was badly burned in the magazine explosion at Fort George on 27 May 1813 – an operation which he commanded in co-operation with Cdre. Oliver H.Perry. Recovering, Scott became a brigadier-general in early 1814, and won the battle of Chippewa (5 July 1814). He was made a major-general at the end of the war.

After the war Scott traveled in Europe for a time; he prepared military manuals, served in wars with the Seminoles and Creeks, and removed the Cherokees from Georgia. In 1841 he was named general-in-chief of the armies of the United States. Politically Scott was a Whig, and when war with Mexico broke out in 1846 the then-President, Polk, did not want to give him any opportunity to win a victory that might make him a presidential candidate. However, fearing that Zachary Taylor was winning just such victories on the Mexican border, he did finally let Scott command a field army. Scott's landings at Vera Cruz (March 1847) opened a masterly six-month campaign during which he drove west from the coast, captured Mexico City against great odds (14 September 1847), and brought the war to a victorious end. Thereafter Scott was indeed nominated as the Whig presidential candidate in 1852, but lost the election. In 1859 he was the United States commissioner who successfully settled a border dispute between the United States and Britain concerning the Canadian border.

The senior ranks of the pre-war army were characterized by extreme old age, and when the Civil War broke out Scott was well past his prime. Nonetheless, his military mind was still sharp. He wrote to the new administration's Secretary of State on 3 March 1861 that the seceding states could be conquered, but it would take "two or three years, a young and able general – a Wolfe, a Dessaix, or a Hoche – with three hundred thousand disciplined men (kept up to that number), estimating a third for garrison, and the loss of a yet greater number by skirmishes, sieges, battles, and Southern fevers. The destruction of life and property on the other side would be frightful – however perfect the moral discipline of the invaders." At this time Scott was virtually the only individual on the continent who foresaw what such a war would entail; most leaders predicted a short fight with little cost.

However, since it was determined that the Federal government would fight to keep the country together, Scott drew up a plan to win the war. This called for a naval blockade of Southern ports, an army drive to open the Mississippi to split the Confederacy in half, and then the crushing of the rebellion piecemeal. This appreciation, called the "Anaconda Plan", eventually formed the basis of the Federal war effort and, indeed, won the war.

On 30 December 1860, Scott had written to President Buchanan an apology for sending a note with ideas on the national crisis, adding, "It is Sunday, the weather is bad, and General Scott [he habitually referred to himself in the third person] is not well enough even to go to church." Finally, he wrote in his memoirs: "A cripple, unable to walk without assistance for three years, Scott, on retiring from all military

When the Civil War broke out the US Army had only four line officers of general rank: Winfield Scott (illustrated), David E.Twigg, John E.Wool, and William S.Harney. The last named was the only one under 70 years of age, and the only one who had not fought in the War of 1812. Winfield Scott had been directly commissioned into the army by President Jefferson in 1808, and had earned his first general's star in the War of 1812. When the Civil War broke out he had already been the army's commanding general for 20 years.

Scott and his staff in full dress. By 1861 he was 74 years old, grossly fat, and infirm to the point of being unable to ride and hardly able to walk. Nevertheless, the aged victor of Chippewa, Cerro Gordo, Churubusco and Chapultepec designed the strategy that eventually won the Civil War. Possibly America's greatest soldier, Scott lived to see Union victory before dying at West Point in 1866.

duty, October 31, 1861 – being broken down by official labors of from nine to seventeen hours a day, with a decided tendency to vertigo and dropsy, I had the honor to be waited on by President Lincoln, at the head of his Cabinet, who, in a neat and affecting address, took leave of the worn-out soldier." After retirement Winfield Scott went abroad for a short time before settling at West Point, where he died on 29 May 1866, having lived long enough to see victory achieved more or less as he had predicted. He lies in the Post Cemetery at the Academy.

SEDGWICK, John (1813–64)

John Sedgwick (**see Plate H2**) was born at Cornwall Hollow, Connecticut, on 13 September 1813. After early education at a local school and Sharon Academy he went to West Point, where he was graduated in 1837. Thereafter he fought against the Seminoles and participated in the removal of the Cherokees from Georgia. During the Mexican War he served under both Zachary Taylor and Winfield Scott, winning brevets as captain and major.

In 1855 Sedgwick was named major of the new 1st US Cavalry, under Col. Robert E.Lee. When his two immediate superiors resigned to join the Confederate Army in 1861 Sedgwick became the regiment's senior officer. He was commissioned brigadier-general of volunteers on 31 August 1861, commanding a division in II Corps in the Peninsula campaign, where he was badly wounded at Glendale (30 June 1862). Promoted to major-general of volunteers on 4 July 1862, he returned to fight at Antietam (17 September), where he was wounded three times and carried unconscious from the field.

Recovering after only three months, he returned to command IX Corps for a short time before being switched to VI Corps. Sedgwick was then discussed as a potential commander of the Army of the Potomac. On 28 April 1863 Marsena Patrick confided in his diary: "Sedgwick, I fear, is not enough of a General for that position – He is a good honest fellow & that is all. I do not think his officers have much confidence in him."

Sedgwick served at Chancellorsville (1–6 May 1863), but his corps was largely in reserve at Gettysburg (1–3 July 1863). In November 1863 he was given temporary command of both VI and V Corps for an operation in which they captured some 1,700 prisoners, eight flags, and four cannon at Rappahannock Bridge. His corps fought well in the Wilderness (5–6 May 1864). On 9 May, at Spotsylvania, he was warned against exposing himself while posting his troops. His famous reply was, "They couldn't hit an elephant at this distance" – a remark followed immediately by the thud of a bullet hitting him below the left eye and killing him almost instantly. He was buried in Cornwall Hollow. Grant later wrote of him:

"Sedgwick was killed at Spotsylvania before I had an opportunity of forming an estimate of his qualifications as a soldier from personal observation. I had known him in Mexico when both of us were lieutenants, and when our service gave no indication that either of us would ever be equal to the command of a brigade. He stood very high in the army, however, as an officer and a man. He was brave and conscientious. His ambition was not great, and he seemed to dread responsibility. He was willing to do any amount of battling, but always wanted some one else to direct."

John Sedgwick, standing at the center of the bottom step with his hand tucked into his coat, seems never to have desired independent command, but was rapidly promoted to lead a corps in the Peninsula campaign and at Antietam. Frank Haskell wrote: "Sedgwick is quite a heavy man, short, thick-set and muscular, with florid complexion, dark, calm, straight-looking eyes, with full, heavyish features, which, with his eyes, have plenty of animation when he is aroused. He has a magnificent profile, well cut, with the nose and forehead forming almost a straight line, curly, short, chestnut hair and full beard, cut short, with a little gray in it. He dresses carelessly, but can look magnificently when he is well dressed. Like Meade, he looks and is, honest and modest. You might see at once, why his men, because they love him, call him 'Uncle John', not to his face, of course, but among themselves."

SHERIDAN, Philip Henry (1831–88)

Philip Sheridan **(see Plate G3)** was born in Albany, New York, on 6 March 1831, but his family soon moved to Somerset, Ohio. There Sheridan acquired his basic education and clerked in a general store, before being appointed to the West Point class of 1852. While at the Academy he was suspended for a year for fighting with a fellow cadet, hence graduating in 1853, in the bottom third of his class. He was appointed to the 4th US Infantry, and served thereafter on the frontier.

Coming East at the outbreak of the Civil War, he served on Gen. Henry Halleck's staff, before being appointed chief quartermaster and commissary of the Army of Southwest Missouri. Although Sheridan's hard work kept that army well maintained, he and his army commander

Philip Sheridan, an infantry officer before the war, earned command of the 2nd Michigan Cavalry in the West; he did so well in that and higher commands that Grant brought him East to command the cavalry of the Army of the Potomac. Seen here toward the end of the war, Sheridan was supremely self-confident, and with reason. Energetic and ruthless, he would eventually become the US Army's general-in-chief in 1883, living just long enough to receive the rank of full general five years later.

did not see eye to eye. Halleck transferred him back to his own headquarters just before he was court-martialed. There Sheridan caught the eye of some superiors, including William T.Sherman, who saw that he was given command of the 2nd Michigan Cavalry. From this point on Sheridan conducted himself so well that he became one of the bright lights of the Union army.

He was made a brigadier-general of volunteers on 13 September 1862, and saw hard fighting at Perryville (8 October) and Murfreesboro (31 December 1862–3 January 1863). On 16 March 1863 Sheridan was promoted major-general, ranking from the date of Murfreesboro. He commanded a division of XX Corps at Chickamauga (19–20 September 1863), losing some 1,500 men out of the 4,000 under his command. After being besieged in Chattanooga, it was Sheridan's men who stormed Missionary Ridge and hurled the Confederates south (25 November 1863). Ulysses S.Grant, now on the scene in Tennessee, was suitably impressed. When Grant came East he brought in Sheridan to take over the cavalry of the Army of the Potomac, whose previous commanders had lackluster records.

Colonel J.H.Kidd, 6th Michigan Cavalry, described Sheridan as he saw him first when the newcomer assumed this command: "There was nothing about Sheridan's appearance at first glance to mark him as the principal figure in the scene... He was well mounted and sat his horse like a real cavalryman. Though short in stature he did not appear so on horseback. His stirrups were high up, the shortness being of leg and not of trunk. He wore a peculiar style hat not like that of any other officer. He was square of shoulder and there was plenty of room for the display of a major-general's buttons on his broad chest. His face was strong, with a firm jaw, a keen eye, and extraordinary firmness in every lineament. In his manner there was an alertness, evinced rather in look than in movement. Nothing escaped his eye, which was brilliant and searching and at the same time emitted flashes of kindly good nature. When riding among or past his troopers, he had a way of casting quick, comprehensive glances to the right and left and in all directions. He overlooked nothing. One had a feeling that he was under close and critical observation, that Sheridan had his eye on him was mentally taking his measure and would remember and recognize him the next time."

Sheridan's vastly stronger cavalry manhandled the smaller and less well supplied Confederate cavalry in the 1864 campaign, striking deep into the enemy's rear areas. As a result, Grant gave him command of the army sent against Jubal Early in the Shenandoah Valley after Early's "Washington Raid". Sheridan, given orders to clear the Valley once and for all, defeated Early in battle after battle between August 1864 and March 1865. Early struck at Cedar Creek (19 October) while

Sheridan was recognized by his men by the odd little black hat that he wore. On 19 October 1864 he rode along the lines of troops driven from their positions at Cedar Creek by Jubal Early, rallying them to hold and then leading them back into the attack that eventually gained one of the most overwhelming victories of the war.

Sheridan was away in Washington, but the latter returned in the nick of time to rally his troops and virtually destroy the Confederate force.

With the Valley essentially Union, Sheridan was made a major-general in the regular army on 14 November 1864, and rejoined the Army of the Potomac at Petersburg. In command of both the cavalry and an infantry corps, he continued pressing Lee's battered Army of Northern Virginia in the Appomattox campaign of April 1865, preventing the Confederates from joining forces in North Carolina and thus forcing Lee's surrender.

After the war Sheridan was given command of the Fifth Military District in the southwest, where he treated the defeated Southerners so harshly that he was recalled after only six months. Thereafter he held a number of commands, and success in the Cheyenne and Pawnee campaign of 1868–69 brought him promotion to lieutenant-general. In 1870–71 he followed the Franco-Prussian War as an observer. In November 1883 he became general-in-chief of the US Army; named a full general on 1 June 1888, he died only two months later on 5 August at Nonquitt, Massachusetts. He is buried in Arlington National Cemetery.

SICKLES, Daniel Edgar (1819–1914)

Daniel Sickles (**see Plate E3**) was born on 20 October 1819 in New York City. He attended New York University and studied law thereafter. Advancing through Democratic Party politics, he served as the city's corporation counsel, first secretary of the London legation, New York state senator, and US Representative. In 1859 Sickles discovered that his wife was having an affair with Philip Barton Key (son of the author of *The Star Spangled Banner*), whereupon he shot Key dead in broad daylight within yards of the White House. In one of the most sensational trials of the century his counsel, Edwin M.Stanton (later Secretary of War), had Sickles plead temporary insanity, the first time such a defense had ever been offered in the United States. Sickles was acquitted; but it was his defiance of the conventions of the time in taking his tarnished wife back that led to his being ostracized by polite society. In an open letter to the press Sickles declared that he was unaware "of any statute or code of morals which makes it infamous to forgive a woman."

Sickles would never escape his notoriety. Charles Haydon, an officer in the 2nd Michigan, recalled in his diary on 28 February 1862 a conversation with a local civilian near the picket line. "He wanted to know last night if I had heard abt that

Daniel Sickles, a shady New York lawyer and politician who dabbled in militia affairs, was given a general's commission to prove that Democrats supported the Republican administration in the Civil War. Not a professional soldier, he wears here a comfortable, informal version of the general's uniform. Sickles was certainly no coward (he smoked a cigar while being carried from the field with a smashed leg at Gettysburg), and seems to have been an effective leader at a junior level, but he was unfitted to command a corps.

murder in Washington. I asked him what one. "Why abt that – that whats his name – Sickles, who shot a man (Keys) the other day". He overheard some of the pickets talking abt it & having never heard of it before concluded it must be a new thing."

At the outbreak of war Sickles, who had earlier served in the New York militia, resigned from Congress to return to New York and raise the Excelsior Brigade. He was named a brigadier-general of volunteers from 3 September 1861, and was given command of the brigade, thus demonstrating Democratic Party support for the war. Showing great personal bravery and some aptitude for command, he was named a major-general ranking from 29 November 1862. He had command of a division on the Peninsula, at Antietam and Fredericksburg in 1862, and of III Corps at Fredericksburg and Gettysburg.

Very few of his fellow generals thought much of Sickles, however. The waspish Marsena Patrick noted in April 1863: "Sickles & the most of his crew, are poor – very poor concerns in my opinion." Staff officer Frank Haskell, writing about Gettysburg, said that he thought that there "General Sickles supposed he was doing for the best; but he was neither born nor bred a soldier. But one can scarcely tell what may have been the motives of such a man – a politician, and some other things, exclusive of the *Barton Key* affair – a man after show and notoriety, and newspaper fame, and the adulation of the mob!"

At Gettysburg (2 July 1863), dissatisfied with the spot in the line where he had been placed, Sickles advanced his corps to what he saw as better ground. Hardly had he done so when his line was struck by the main Confederate attack. While attempting to rally his men he was shot in the right leg and carried away, nonchalantly smoking a cigar. His leg was amputated, and he never returned to command, although he stayed in the regular army as a major-general until retiring in 1869.

Sickles was later appointed minister to Spain, where he apparently tried to get the two countries into a war over the Spanish capture of an American boat, the *Virginius*, which was running guns into Cuba in 1873. Cooler heads prevailed and a compromise was worked out over his head. He then served in Congress in 1893–95, and was chairman of the New York State Monuments Commission. In 1912 he was removed from the commission for alleged peculation. Slipping into mental illness in his final years, he died at last on 3 May 1914 in New York, and is buried in Arlington National Cemetery.

STONEMAN, George (1822–94)

George Stoneman (**see Plate G1**) was born in Busti, New York, on 22 August 1822. Educated at Jamestown Academy, he went on to West Point where he was graduated in 1846 – George McClellan was a classmate – and was commissioned into the 1st Dragoons. During the Mexican War he was the quartermaster for the Mormon Battalion on its

Although his bungling threatened the integrity of the Union line on the second day of Gettysburg, Sickles was probably most notorious for his private life. He had shot his wife's lover dead in broad daylight, successfully pleaded temporary insanity as a defense at the subsequent trial, and publically forgave his wife thereafter.

George Stoneman, standing center wearing from left shoulder to right hip the sash which indicates that he was serving as general officer of the day. He and his staff pose here in April 1863; a month later he would lead the Army of the Potomac's cavalry off on a fruitless raid during the Chancellorsville campaign.

march from Leavenworth, Kansas, to San Diego, California. At the outbreak of the Civil War he was a captain in the 2nd Cavalry – suffering, as a result of years in the saddle, from a chronic case of hemorrhoids.

Stoneman was quickly placed on McClellan's staff as a major. Commissioned a brigadier-general of volunteers on 13 August 1861, he was named chief of cavalry of the Army of the Potomac (essentially a staff post with no real command functions) when McClellan became army commander. During the Peninsula campaign he actually commanded an infantry division in III Corps, but during much of the campaign he was unable to ride because of sickness, which limited his activities. Even so, made a major-general of volunteers dating from 29 November 1862, he commanded III Corps at Fredericksburg (13 December).

When Hooker took over the Army of the Potomac, Stoneman was made chief of cavalry in a reorganization that made the army's cavalry an effective, independent organization – something he had unsuccessfully urged upon McClellan. He was sent with the Cavalry Corps to raid the rear of the Army of Northern Virginia during the Chancellorsville campaign of May 1863. One fellow general, while awaiting news of the results of a Stoneman raid, said, "I know Stoneman like a book. He will go to the proper spot like a cannon-ball, but when he gets there, like a shell he'll burst." Indeed, the only practical effect of this raid was to deprive the main army of its intelligence-gathering capacities when it needed them most.

After Chancellorsville, and as a result of this poor performance, Stoneman was replaced on 22 May by Alfred Pleasonton. After a time as chief of the Cavalry Bureau in Washington he was returned to a combat command in the winter of 1864. Given XXIII Corps, he actually commanded the Cavalry Corps of the Army of the Ohio during the Atlanta campaign. There his performance was again lackluster. Major-General David Stanley, who had earlier been chief of cavalry of the Army of the Cumberland, told a US Christian Commission delegate that Stoneman was "not competent to command a company."

Stoneman was captured on 31 July 1864 during a raid aimed at freeing prisoners kept at Camp Sumter near Andersonville, Georgia, at the head of two brigades serving as a rear guard to cover the escape of the rest of his command. That October he was exchanged, and commanded troops in eastern Tennessee, northwestern North Carolina, and southwestern Virginia during the last days of the war.

After the war Stoneman was breveted a major-general but assigned as colonel commanding the 21st US Infantry. He commanded the Department of Arizona until retirement in 1871. He then moved to an estate at San Marino, California, serving as railroad commissioner and a term as governor of California in 1882. He died in Buffalo, New York, on 5 September 1894, and was buried at Lakewood, New York.

SUMNER, Edwin Vose (1797–1863)

Edwin Sumner (see **Plate B3**) was born on 30 January 1797 in Boston. Commissioned directly as a lieutenant in the 2nd US Infantry in 1819, he was made a captain of dragoons in 1833, and served largely on the frontier. In 1846 he was promoted to major and saw service in Mexico, winning two brevets and promotion to lieutenant-colonel in 1848. Named colonel of the 1st Cavalry in 1855, he saw service as commander of Fort Leavenworth during the Kansas troubles.

In 1861 he was named a brigadier-general to replace David Twigg, who had gone south. On the creation of corps in the Army of the Potomac, Sumner was given command of II Corps, which he led in the Peninsula campaign despite receiving two wounds. At first he was not especially effective, McClellan privately writing after the battle of Williamsburg (5 May 1862), "Sumner had proved that he was even a greater fool than I had supposed & had come within an ace of having us defeated." However, after the action at Fair Oaks (31 May–1 June), McClellan wrote to Secretary of War Edwin Stanton that Sumner "displayed the utmost energy in bringing his troops into action, & handled them with the utmost courage in action. He repulsed every attack of the enemy, & drove him wherever he could get at him."

Sumner was breveted a major-general for his service at Fair Oaks on 31 May 1862, and named a major-general of volunteers on 16 July. In August, however, Charles Wainwright recorded a rumor in the army that "General Sumner is said to be very feeble, and failing fast; he has never got over the severe fall from his horse he had last winter." This was not true, as Sumner went on to serve at Antietam (17 September), where there was some complaint that he led his head division like a cavalry colonel rather than a corps commander, who should have been in the rear to supervise. Nevertheless, he was given command of the Left Grand Division, consisting of II and IX Corps, at Fredericksburg in December.

When Hooker was given command of the Army of the Potomac, Sumner asked to be relieved. On his way to his new command, the Department of the Missouri, he died at Syracuse, New York, on 21 March

1863. He is buried in the Oakwood Cemetery there. Writing after his death, Marsena Patrick noted that Sumner "was a mere soldier – a man of the world & nothing but a man of the world... ." Wainwright was harsher, writing on hearing of Sumner's death: "Owing to his incompetence to fill so large a post as corps commander, we lost the chance to destroy Johnston's army at Williamsburg last May, Antietam was but half a victory; and the heights of Fredericksburg were not secured in December when we first came here.

"But the old soldier was as honest as the day, and simple as a child. The fault was not so much his, as of those who put him and kept him in such a place, while the glorious way in which he pushed across the half-gone bridges to the relief of Keyes at Fair Oaks suffices to cover all his faults."

THE PLATES: EAST

The regulation uniform of a general officer was a double-breasted dark blue frock coat with a dark blue velvet standing collar and round "jam pot" cuffs. Major-generals had two rows of nine buttons arranged in groups of three; brigadier-generals had two rows of eight buttons arranged in pairs. Rank was also indicated by transverse shoulder straps of dark blue velvet edged with gold embroidery, bearing two silver stars for a major-general and one for a brigadier-general. The cap or hat badge was a black velvet oval with a gold embroidered wreath enclosing "U.S." in silver Old English lettering. For full dress, gold braid epaulettes were worn, with heavy gold fringes, and two or one silver stars.

The trousers were plain dark blue. The general officers' sword was straight, with a gilt guard, black leather grip wrapped with gilt wire, and a black scabbard with brass mounts. The full dress sword had a silver grip and a brass or steel scabbard. The sword knot was of gold cord with an acorn end. In the field a black leather belt was worn with a plain gilt plate showing the arms of the United States. The full dress belt was of red leather with lengthways gold braid stripes. For dress, and occasionally in the field, a buff silk tasseled sash was worn under the belt.

It should be emphasized that this was the regulation uniform; in practice generals wore variations to suit their needs and preferences.

Irvin McDowell (left) as commander of I Corps, with his army commander George McClellan, before the 1862 Peninsula campaign. Lincoln insisted that McDowell's corps be left behind to protect Washington; McClellan subsequently used this excuse to point the finger of blame at Lincoln for the campaign's failure. Note McDowell's odd forage cap, taller than usual and standing straight like a shako. Distrusting his loyalty, after First Bull Run some soldiers in his army actually claimed that this odd hat marked him out in the field so that Confederates, who knew he was secretly aiding them, would not accidentally shoot him!

Ambrose Burnside wore his old Rhode Island "sack" even when he was a general officer, along with a version of the US Army dress hat stripped of its embroidery and feathers – see Plate C2.

A: MAY 1861
A1: Major-General Commanding the Army Winfield Scott
A2: Major-General Benjamin Butler
A3: Brigadier-General Irvin McDowell

Three generals who were important in the early days of the war meet in Washington to discuss that city's defense. At the outset there was considerable fear that the capital, surrounded by the slave-holding states of Maryland and Virginia, would fall to Southern forces. There were only some 55 officers and men of the Ordnance Corps, and 300 to 400 Marines stationed within city limits, and some of the city's militia companies were of suspect loyalty. Benjamin Butler led some of the first troops from New England to defend Washington; his immediate appointment as a major-general of volunteers was politically motivated. Scott and McDowell, both professional soldiers, were already in the capital. Scott would be obliged to retire on grounds of age and health, while both McDowell and Butler would be disgraced by subsequent failures.

Scott (A1), known to his men as "Old Fuss and Feathers", and Butler both preferred fanciful variations on regulation dress; note the heavy gold embroidery on the fall collar and cuffs affected by Scott. Unique in his rank as Major-General Commanding the Army, Scott wore its three silver stars on his epaulettes, the center star larger than the other two. Eventually the three-star insignia would be adopted for use by Ulysses S.Grant when he was named a lieutenant-general, and would survive as a lieutenant-general's rank insignia to this day. Butler (A2) has the regulation stand collar, but also sports gold embroidery along its top and front edges; portraits show at least two variations of this style. McDowell (A3) preferred regulation dress, but was unmistakable for his unique style of cap – see accompanying photograph.

B: AUGUST 1862
B1: Major-General John Pope
B2: Major-General Fitz John Porter
B3: Major-General Edwin Sumner

Toward the end of his disastrous Second Bull Run (Manassas) campaign, John Pope, commanding the Army of Virginia, meets two Army of the Potomac corps commanders, while in the background exhausted men of John Gibbon's "Iron Brigade" prepare their suppers. All three wear the regulation uniform for major-generals, differenced only by their personal choice of headgear; Porter (B2) wears the so-called "McClellan" style forage cap, the other two broad-brimmed slouch hats with gold cord and acorns, Sumner's (B3) without a badge. Pope would later have Porter court-martialed; he was always bitter about what he believed was the desire of senior officers of the Army of the Potomac to see him beaten in the field. He wrote years later: "It was the knowledge of this feeling and the open exultation of Franklin and other officers of rank in his corps over the fact that their comrades had been worsted in the battle of the day before which induced me to recommend that the army be drawn back to the intrenchments around Washington and there thoroughly reorganized. There did not appear to me to be any hope of success for that army while such a feeling prevailed among so many of its higher officers."

C: NOVEMBER 1862
C1: Major-General George McClellan
C2: Major-General Ambrose Burnside
C3: Brigadier-General Henry Hunt

McClellan turns over command of the Army of the Potomac to Ambrose Burnside, 7 November 1862. It was well after dark when Burnside arrived with Gen. Catharinus Buckingham, who had been on duty at the War Department at the time and personally delivered the orders from the Secretary of War to Burnside; a newspaper sketch artist caught McClellan and Burnside in discussion outside the former's headquarters tent. McClellan, who had constantly misread Abraham Lincoln, was shocked to receive orders to hand over command; but he wisely disregarded the excitable advice of his supporters in the army to ignore them. Instead he retired to Trenton, New Jersey (which one wag said was the only city he was able to take). McClellan described the event in a letter to his wife written at 11.30pm that night:

"No cause is given. I am ordered to turn over the command immediately & repair to Trenton N.J. & on my arrival there to report by telegraph for future orders!! Poor Burn feels dreadfully, almost crazy – I am sorry for him, & he never showed himself a better man or truer friend than now. Of course I was much surprised – but as I read the order in the presence of Genl Buckingham, I am sure that not a muscle quivered nor was the slightest expression of feeling visible on my face, which he watched closely. They shall not have that triumph. They have made a great mistake – alas for my poor country – I know in my innermost heart she never had a truer servant. I have informally turned over the command to Burnside – but will go tomorrow to Warrenton with him, & perhaps remain a day or two there in order to give him all the information in my power."

While McClellan **(C1)** wears entirely regulation uniform with the style of forage cap named after him and tall black riding boots, Burnside **(C2)** still wears his old Rhode Island militia overshirt, which he preferred to wear in the field even as an army commander; the other details of his costume are also from photographs. Inside the tent, Gen.Hunt **(C3)**, the army's brilliant chief of artillery, wears a custom-made single-breasted fatigue blouse with a fall collar, and a black rubberized rain cover on his cap.

D: MAY 1863
D1: Major-General Joseph Hooker
D2: Major-General Darius Couch
D3: Major-General William Franklin

Hooker, Burnside's successor as commander of the Army of the Potomac, meets with his second in command, Couch, and the commander of VI Corps, Franklin, before the Chancellorsville campaign, as his troops form up to get under way; the infantry regiment in the background is led by its fife and drum corps. Note the regulation horse furniture for a general officer **(D1)**. All three generals wear regulation uniform, but note that Couch **(D2)** is shown in photographs with major-general's shoulder straps applied to his old brigadier-general's coat.

During the campaign Darius Couch would become disgusted with Hooker, who he believed to have lost all confidence and who, instead of following the original plan to burst out of the Wilderness in Lee's rear, withdrew to defensive lines around the Chancellor House, only to meet decisive defeat there.

E: JUNE 1863
E1: Major-General George Meade
E2: Major-General John Reynolds
E3: Major-General Daniel Sickles

Just before Gettysburg, the new Army of the Potomac commander Gen.Meade discusses Lee's invasion of Pennsylvania with Reynolds, commander of I Corps, and Sickles, commander of III Corps; in the background troops have set up an evening camp. Meade gave Reynolds command of all the troops on the scene on the first day of the battle, but Reynolds was killed while scouting that afternoon. Sickles would put the Union line at risk through his unauthorized movement of his command just before the Confederates struck on the second day; Gettysburg would cost him a leg, but he would live to a ripe old age, surrounded by an aura of rascality. All three generals are taken from photographs. Note Sickles' **(E3)** open single-breasted coat worn over a waistcoat, with his major-general's stars worn on shoulder straps lacking the regulation gold borders. Many of Meade's personal effects survive in the Civil War Library & Museum, Philadelphia, PA; he was portrayed with a dress sword belt of red leather with gold braid stripes.

F: II CORPS COMMANDERS, AUTUMN 1864
F1: Major-General Winfield Scott Hancock
F2: Brigadier-General Francis Barlow
F3: Brigadier-General John Gibbon

The greatly admired Gen. Hancock sits with two of the divisional commanders of his II Corps in 1864 – after a famous photograph (from which we have omitted Maj.Gen. David Birney) of a group of generals all of whom had been wounded at Gettysburg the previous year. Hancock **(F1)**, whose life was despaired of at one point, wears regulation uniform but without a hat badge. Barlow **(F2)** had been so badly wounded that he was left for dead, but had recovered enough to rejoin the army for the 1864 campaign. He wears the plain, single-breasted short jacket preferred as more comfortable than a frock coat in the saddle, and a standard issue cavalry saber. Instead of the regulation "U.S." he displays the single silver star of his rank on the front of his issue forage cap. Gibbon **(F3)**, an artilleryman before the war and author of *The Artillerist's Manual* while an instructor at West Point, was the second commander of the "Iron Brigade" of troops from Wisconsin, Indiana, and Michigan. Here he wears a custom-made version of the fatigue blouse or "sack coat" and the single star of brigadier-general – he was promoted major-general from early June. Note the use of civilian shirts under the uniform coats.

G: CAVALRY COMMANDERS OF THE ARMY OF THE POTOMAC
G1: Brigadier-General George Stoneman
G2: Major-General Alfred Pleasonton
G3: Major-General Philip Sheridan

The cavalry of the Army of the Potomac was commanded successively by these three officers, all of whom wear largely regulation uniform for their rank, and carry plain cavalry sabers. The only striking detail is Sheridan's **(G3)** odd hat, a small black felt rather resembling a straw boater in outline. Neither Pleasonton nor Stoneman proved very successful in the field; but Stoneman did successfully lobby to make the

Cavalry Corps a separate, independent command instead of splitting it up among various infantry corps – an important factor in its later success under Philip Sheridan. By the time Sheridan took command the quality of the Confederate cavalry, in terms of horses, weapons, and numbers, was so relatively poor that he easily outfought them in most engagements.

H: PETERSBURG, MAY 1864
H1: Major-General Andrew Humphreys
H2: Major-General John Sedgwick
H3: Major-General Joshua Chamberlain

In front of Army of the Potomac headquarters in the field, Gen. Chamberlain reports to the army chief-of-staff, Gen. Humphreys. Andrew Humphreys made the successful transition from topographical engineer to unit commander to army chief-of-staff, where his work was quite successful, and then to corps commander, marking him as a superior

soldier. He wears regulation uniform **(H1)** with his trousers outside his boots.

John Sedgwick **(H2)** was one of the army's most beloved corps commanders; although his superiors found him unwilling to assume independent command responsibility, his death at Spotsylvania on 9 May was a real blow to the army. His saddle and other effects are preseved in the West Point Museum; a photograph shows him with his coat worn open at the neck. The Maine general Joshua Chamberlain **(H3)**, the hero of Little Round Top, is illustrated here resplendent in as near to a dress uniform as would be worn in the field, where epaulettes were virtually never seen; he has the general's buff sash beneath his plain black belt supporting a staff officer's sword. This remarkable officer became more widely known through the pages of Michael Shaara's Pulitzer prize-winning 1975 novel *The Killer Angels*, which later formed the basis for the 1993 feature film *Gettysburg*.

Joseph Hooker – see Plate D1 – certainly looked the part of a general. His estimation of his own worth was not shared by his contemporaries such as John Gibbon and Ulysses Grant, however; and when he threatened to resign after being passed over for a command, Gen.Sherman calmly let this disloyal subordinate go.

PART 2
UNION LEADERS IN THE WEST

INTRODUCTION

THE SO-CALLED WESTERN THEATER of the Civil War, which actually covers everything from Kentucky and Tennessee all the way to New Mexico, produced the Union Army's best generals. One advantage they enjoyed was that most of the media was in the East and concentrated on military activities along the Atlantic seaboard. Consequently Western generals often had time to develop their talents free from close public scrutiny. Minor setbacks such as the battle of Belmont, where Grant blooded his troops and staff for the first time, were not magnified by the press into the 'important' tests that made or broke Eastern generals' reputations before they had a chance to develop.

Most of the major Union generals in the West had been trained as professional soldiers at the US Military Academy at West Point, New York, although – like their colleagues elsewhere – none had ever before exercised senior command in the field. They included, however, a handful of political leaders appointed to positions of command by the

William T.Sherman – seated in carved chair, center – who exercised overall Union command in the Western theater in 1864–65, with six of his subordinate generals. From left to right: Oliver O.Howard, John A.Logan, William B.Hazen; Jefferson C.Davis, Henry W.Slocum, and J.A.Mower. (*Battles and Leaders of the Civil War*)

Lincoln administration in order to show the American public that the war had broad-based political support from all the parties. At times these appointees – such as Francis Blair and "Black Jack" Logan – performed well. Other political generals – such as Nathaniel Prentiss Banks – were incapable of leading a detail on a latrine-cleaning operation. All too often professional and political generals did not get along together at all well, much to the detriment of the war effort.

Generals supervised their commands through their staffs. These staffs were considerably smaller than later armies would regard as the necessary minimum. According to one of Grant's staff officers, Horace Porter, only 14 men made up Grant's staff when he was overall commander of the Union Army. These comprised Brig.Gen. John A.Rawlins as chief-of-staff; four lieutenant-colonels as aides-de-camp (including Grant's brother-in-law); two lieutenant-colonels serving as military secretaries; a lieutenant-colonel as assistant adjutant general, backed by two captains (one of them the full-blooded Native-American Eli S.Parker); a lieutenant-colonel as assistant inspector general; a captain as assistant quartermaster; and a lieutenant to act as aide-de-camp to the chief-of-staff. Finally, a volunteer from Iowa named Peter T.Hudson, who had served with Grant early on, was retained and given the rank of captain. With appropriately lower ranks for the staff officers, this was the basic structure found among the staffs of lower level commands.

One of Sherman's staff officers, George Ward Nichols, recalled: "His staff is smaller than that of any brigade commander in the army. He has fewer servants and horses than the military regulations allow; his baggage is reduced to the smallest possible limit; he sleeps in a fly-tent like the rest of us, rejecting the effeminacy of a house; and the soldier in the ranks indulges in luxuries (the fruits of some daring forage raid, to be sure) which his chief never sees."

BIOGRAPHIES: WEST

BANKS, Nathaniel Prentiss (1816–94)

Nathaniel P.Banks (**see Plate B1**) was born at Waltham, Massachusetts, on 30 January 1816. From a poor family, he had to go to work as a child at a cotton mill – which later gave rise to his nickname, "The Bobbin Boy of Massachusetts." Although he received little in the way of formal education, he managed to learn enough to be admitted to the bar when he was 23 years old. Thereafter he pursued a political career. He ran for the Massachusetts Legislature seven times before finally winning election to that body. Once there, however, his career was brilliant: he became the speaker of the house, president of the Constitutional Convention in 1853, and was elected to the US House of Representatives ten times. In 1856 he was elected speaker of the House of Representatives after a long and bitter campaign in which he stood for the moderate position on issues such as slavery. In 1858 he was elected governor of Massachusetts.

In 1861 Lincoln, needing to have influential Democratic Party representatives involved in the suppression of the rebellion, asked Banks to accept a commission of major-general of volunteers. Banks, who lacked any military qualifications but had been an important supporter of the Lincoln administration's war policy in his state, accepted. As it turned out, this was probably a mistake. Banks proved to be a poor soldier, although he was continually given independent commands. He had a separate command in the Valley of Virginia in 1862, where he was conspicuously outgeneralled by "Stonewall" Jackson. Although he came close to beating Jackson at Cedar Mountain in August 1862, eventually his command was routed there. When he left, John Geary, one of his officers, who at first felt badly used by Banks, wrote home, "I had a liking for Genl B. and in that respect I regret the change, but this must be 'inter nos.'"

Thereafter Banks was sent West to command in Louisiana. He was assigned the job of capturing Port Hudson, where he wasted many Northern lives in useless attempts to force the Confederate fortifications. After the fall of Vicksburg, Port Hudson, having stood off the longest siege ever fought on American soil, was forced to surrender anyway.

Banks then led a campaign along the Red River from Louisiana, ostensibly to capture East Texas but probably as much to capture valuable cotton that could be sold for a large profit to hungry mills in the North. A junior officer in his command in Louisiana in 1864, John William De Forest, noted that, "The truth is that Banks was the most merciless marcher of men that I ever

Nathaniel Prentiss Banks. Note the pocket cut into the left breast of the major-general's frock coat – a typical personal modification – and the large black bow tie worn outside the collar. (*Military Images* magazine)

knew." He noted that during the Red River campaign the soldiers struggling along under a blistering sun were "muttering curses against Banks and the Confederates – those two enemies."

The Red River campaign was a total failure and Banks narrowly escaped with his army intact. At that point, Henry Halleck wrote, "Banks is not competent…." This was the consensus of opinion in Washington, but because of his political stature Banks was not mustered out of service until August 1865, although he was never placed in command of an "independent expedition against the enemy after the Red River campaign. "The truth is Banks is not a soldier," Sherman wrote after the Red River, "he is too intent on reconstruction [of the South after the war]."

Returning to Massachusetts, Banks was quickly returned to Congress, serving five consecutive terms. He also served a term in the Massachusetts Senate, and spent nine years as United States marshal for Massachusetts. He retired after his fifth Congressional term to Waltham, dying there on 1 September 1894. He is buried in Grove Hill Cemetery.

BLAIR, Francis Preston, Jr (1821–75)

The brother of Lincoln's first postmaster general, Francis P. Blair (**see Plate H3**) was born on 19 February 1821 in Lexington, Kentucky, to a politically important family. A Princeton University graduate, he studied law at Transylvania University in Kentucky before going on to practice in partnership with his brother in St Louis in 1842. Appointed attorney

general of the New Mexico Territory at the outbreak of the Mexican War, he later returned to Missouri and a career in politics. He was elected to Congress in 1856 and 1860 on the ticket of the Free-Soil Party, a Union party in that slave state. His formation of Missouri Home Guards and Wide Awakes was vital in saving Missouri for the Union. As a result, Blair was offered a brigadier-general's commission, but declined it to serve as Chairman of the Committee on Military Defense in the 37th Congress. Finally, on 7 August 1861, he accepted a brigadier-general's commission, and promotion to major-general on 29 November.

Grant later recalled: "General F.P.Blair joined me at Milliken's Bend a full-fledged general, without having served in a lower grade. He commanded a division in the campaign. I had known Blair in Missouri, where I voted against him in 1858 when he ran for Congress. I knew him as a frank, positive and generous man, true to his friends even to a fault, but always a leader. I dreaded his coming; I knew from experience that it was more difficult to command two generals desiring to be generals than it was to command one army officered intelligently and with subordination. It affords me the greatest pleasure to record now my agreeable disappointment in respect to his character. There was no man braver than he, nor was there any who obeyed all orders of his superior in rank with more unquestioning alacrity. He was one man as a soldier, another as a politician."

Blair served as a brigade commander during the Vicksburg campaign, and thereafter as commander of XV and XVII Corps during the March to the Sea (November–December 1864) and the March through the Carolinas (February–March 1865). George W.Nichols, of Sherman's staff, noted that Blair's corps was the first to reach Savannah, Blair himself at the head of the corps: "One who had never seen General Blair except in the field as a corps commander would find it difficult to realize that he has occupied so prominent a position in the political arena; for, while it may not be said that he is a born soldier, yet he possesses in a marked degree many of the qualities which constitute a good commander.... Under all circumstances he never loses that perfect coolness and self-command which render him master of the situation and inspire the confidence of the soldiers. This imperturbability never deserts him.... He selects excellent horses, and knows how to ride them. In the army he has the reputation of a kind, generous, discreet, and brave soldier."

Blair resigned from the army in November 1865 and devoted his energy to a cotton plantation in Mississippi. After this venture failed, he returned to Missouri as a moderate politician. As such his nominations to important positions by President Andrew Johnson were rejected by

Francis Preston Blair, Jr, another political general, but one who earned Grant's praise. George W.Nichols, a member of Sherman's staff, described Blair as "one of the most hospitable and popular men of the army... . The General wears a full sandy beard and mustache, which conceal the lower part of his face. His eyes are of a light hazel color, full of humor and good nature – an expression, however, that is somewhat qualified by the overhanging brow, which has a *noli me tangere* air ['let no man touch me'], as much as to say, "If I must fight, it shall be war to the hilt... . In height [he] is about five feet eleven inches. His frame is finely proportioned and he makes a good appearance on horseback." *(Military Images)*

Blair with his staff officers. Although Sherman termed Blair a "disturbing element" in the army at Vicksburg in March 1863, adding, "I wish he was in Congress or a Bar Room, any where but our Army," he nevertheless entrusted him with a senior corps command during the "March to the Sea" eighteen months later. *(Military Images)*

the radical Republican majority of the US Senate. He ran for vice-president in 1868, but the ticket was defeated. Finally named a US Senator in 1871 to fill a vacant position, Blair resigned in 1873 because of poor health. He died in St Louis on 8 July 1875, and is buried in Bellefontaine Cemetery in that city.

BUELL, Don Carlos (1818–98)

Don Carlos Buell (**see Plate C2**) was born on 23 March 1818 in Ohio, but spent most of his childhood at an uncle's home in Lawrenceburg, Indiana. Appointed to West Point, he was graduated 32nd of 44 in the class of 1841, behind Josiah Gorgas – who would become head of the Confederacy's ordnance efforts. After graduation Buell was posted to the 3rd US Infantry in Florida. He went on to serve in the Mexican War (1846–48), being promoted to first lieutenant on 18 June 1846. He was breveted captain that September "for meritorious conduct during the several conflicts at Monterey." Buell was badly wounded on 20 August 1847 at Churubusco, and was breveted major for his behaviour there and at Contreras. He was named his regimental adjutant on 15 February 1847, being assigned to the overall army staff as an assistant adjutant general on 25 January 1848.

After the Mexican War he remained a staff officer, serving at various departments in the West and East. He was appointed a lieutenant-colonel and assistant adjutant general in the Department of the Pacific just before the Civil War broke out. Buell was married to a native of Georgia and at one point owned eight slaves; despite this, he remained

Don Carlos Buell as a major-general. His fellow general John Pope wrote of him: "He was a short, square man, with an immense physique and personal strength. He was very erect, had a dark impressive face and black eyes and from something in his bearing and general appearance always gave the impression that he was a much taller and larger man than he really was...." (Military Images)

loyal to the Union. Returning to Washington, he was commissioned brigadier-general of volunteers on 17 May 1861.

Picked to lead the Army of the Ohio into East Tennessee from Kentucky, Buell wanted to advance via the Cumberland and Tennessee rivers to Nashville rather than moving through Louisville and Knoxville. Despite opposition from the administration, which was concerned about the political situation in eastern Tennessee, he was given approval to do this, and after the fall of Forts Donelson and Henry he took Nashville without a fight.

As it turned out, Buell was not a great success as a commander of volunteer soldiers. An able administrator, he lacked the ability to motivate volunteers, treating them as brusquely as if they were professional soldiers. "I have frequently felt that had he visited his camps more, reviewed his troops more, and shown himself more to his soldiers, a different state of feeling would have existed," noted one of his subordinates, Alexander McCook, in December 1862.

Buell also insisted on strictly upholding the property rights of local civilians, returning slaves to their owners and forbidding his men to forage. At first his troops, who were mostly pro-slavery, agreed with this; but as time wore on and they saw first-hand the disloyalty among slave-holders, they yearned for a harder policy against pro-Southerners. Buell's army became divided between those in favor of a "soft" and a "hard war". Among the latter was Lucius Barber, 15th Illinois Infantry, who called Buell "an imbecile General... [who] allowed the invaders to carry fire, sword and famine in their track and go unpunished."

When he marched to join Grant's army at Pittsburgh Landing, Buell's lucky arrival while Grant's forces were under attack in the battle of Shiloh turned the tide and secured a Union victory. His troops then served in the slow march on Corinth. Promoted to major-general on 22 March 1862, he was ordered to move on Chattanooga with four divisions in June. His advance was forced back when Confederate raiders under John Hunt Morgan broke up his supply route to Louisville. Buell then returned to Kentucky to oppose a Confederate invasion of the state. When Confederate commander Braxton Bragg failed to take Louisville, Buell did, breaking up Confederate invasion plans. Despite this, Halleck was unhappy with Buell and decided to replace him with George Thomas. Buell was so notified on 29 September 1862; however, Thomas declined the appointment, telling Halleck that Buell was about to move against Bragg and that a replacement at that moment would be untimely. Unfortunately word of the potential replacement spread through the Army of the Ohio, further weakening Buell's authority.

Buell and his troops left Louisville on 1 October, heading after Bragg's army. The two sides finally clashed indecisively at Perryville on the 8th; Bragg gave up the field and retreated, but Buell failed to follow up this opportunity. Buell's own troops were as angry about this as were officials in Washington; Major James Connolly was typical, writing in a letter home: "If Buell had done what he might well have done at Perryville, he would have captured the bulk of Bragg's army, and even after the battle, had he used ordinary expedition he might have destroyed it. But, as he says, the battle was not according to his programme, and therefore he chose not to gather the fruits of it."

Buell was relieved from command on 24 October and was replaced by Rosecrans. A military commission investigated his actions after Perryville that November, but made no recommendations. Buell awaited orders for over a year, but none were forthcoming, and as a result he was mustered out of the volunteer service in May 1864 and resigned his regular commission on the first of the following month.

John Pope summed up Buell thus: "Certainly if a man's military capability is to be judged by his ability to organize troops and present them on the field of battle in the highest condition of discipline and effectiveness, General Buell may well be reckoned among the foremost generals of the war; but unfortunately the qualities and qualifications needed to accomplish this result do not imply, necessarily, or even probably, the requisites for a great commander in the field... .

"He was in no respect social in his habits, but appeared always to be self-absorbed. He was extremely reserved in his demeanor and very silent and reticent, if not at times forbidding, in his manners... . He was a student always. I do not mean a student in the college sense, but a steady and close reader of history and books on military subjects and was probably as well posted on military subjects as almost any officer in the army... . He was a man of tremendous passion, which he with evident difficulty kept under control, but his passions were of a generous and manly character and had no quality of vice or meanness. He was... a pure, upright and most honorable man, capable of great things and the victim rather than the author of the misfortunes which overtook him."

Grant later wrote: "General Buell was a brave, intelligent officer, with as much professional pride and ambition of a commendable sort as I ever knew... . He was not given in early life or in mature years to forming intimate acquaintances. He was studious by habit, and commanded the confidence and respect of all who knew him. He was a strict disciplinarian, and perhaps did not distinguish sufficiently between the volunteer who 'enlisted for the war' and the soldier who serves in time of peace... . General Buell became an object of harsh criticism later, some going so far as to challenge his loyalty. No one who knew him ever believed him capable of a dishonorable act, and nothing could be more dishonorable than to accept high rank and command in war and then betray the trust."

Grant wanted Buell restored to duty, perhaps partially in thanks for his actions at Shiloh, but this did not happen. Buell took a position running

Buell as depicted in the 11 January 1862 issue of *Harper's Weekly*. As so often in these woodcuts, the image has been reversed from left to right – note that the coat is buttoned in the wrong direction, and the hair is parted on the right rather than the left as shown in the photograph.

Edward Canby, who would later be one of the very few senior officers to be killed during the Indian Wars. *(Military Images)*

an ironworks and coal mill at Airdrie, Kentucky; he also served for four years as a government pension agent. He died at Airdrie on 19 November 1898, and is buried in the Bellefontaine Cemetery, St Louis.

CANBY, Edward Richard Sprigg (1817–73)

Edward R.S.Canby **(see Plate C3)** was born at Piatt's Landing, Kentucky, on 9 November 1817. He attended local schools before going to Wabash College, Crawfordsville, Indiana. He was then appointed to West Point, from where he was graduated 30th – next to the bottom – of the class of 1839, the same year as Henry Halleck. As a second lieutenant in the 2nd Infantry he saw service against the Seminoles, Creeks, Cherokees, and Choctaws. In the Mexican War (1846–48) he served on a brigade staff but still received brevets to captain and major for his actions at Contreras and Churubusco, and a lieutenant-colonel's brevet for gallant conduct at the Belen Gate, Mexico City, in 1847. Canby became a major in the 10th Infantry in 1855; he was named colonel of the new 19th Infantry on 14 May 1861, and given command of the Department of New Mexico.

Canby's department had little in the way of troops or supplies, being considered a backwater of the war. Nonetheless the Confederates invaded his domain, on what they planned to be their way to the silver mines of Colorado and the gold mines of California, in January 1862. His outnumbered troops fell back from Valverde, destroying resources upon whose capture the Confederate plan depended. Finally, reinforced by Colorado volunteers, he met the Confederates at Glorieta (called "the Gettysburg of the West"), and destroyed their supplies. The Confederates were forced to fall back all the way to Texas; Canby followed them, not needing to fight again since nature itself was going against them.

On 23 May 1862 he was named a brigadier-general of volunteers and sent East to serve largely in staff functions, although he did take command at New York City during the draft riots of July 1863. He was named major-general of volunteers on 7 May 1864, and given command of the Military Division of West Mississippi. He reorganized the army which had suffered so much under Banks in the Red River campaign, and began the capture of Mobile, Alabama. Mobile surrendered to his forces on 12 April 1865; Canby then accepted the surrender of the forces under Gen Richard Taylor, one of the last large Confederate armies in the field.

In 1866 Canby was named a regular army brigadier-general. In 1870 he was given command of the Department of Columbia, and three years later of the Division of the Pacific. It was on 11 April 1873, in the lava beds of northern California, while negotiating with the Modoc Indians for their removal, that he was suddenly shot through the head and stabbed by several of the Native-American negotiators, including their chief "Captain Jack". Canby was killed on the spot; his body was buried in Crown Hill Cemetery, Indianapolis, Indiana.

Grant later recalled that "General Canby was an officer of great merit. He was naturally studious, and inclined to the law. There have been in the army but very few, if any, officers who took as much interest in reading and digesting every act of Congress and every regulation for the government of the army as he. His knowledge gained in this way made him a most valuable staff officer, a capacity in which almost all his army services were rendered up to the time of his being assigned to the Military Division of the Gulf. He was an exceedingly modest officer, though of great talent and learning... . His character was as pure as his talent and learning were great. His services were valuable during the war, but principally as a bureau officer. I have no idea that it was from choice that his services were rendered in an office, but because of his superior efficiency there."

CURTIS, Samuel Ryan (1805–66)

Samuel R.Curtis **(see Plate A1)** was born in Clinton County, New York, on 3 February 1805, the son of a Connecticut veteran of the Revolutionary War. Shortly afterwards his family moved to Ohio, from where he was appointed to West Point. Graduated 27th of 33 in the class of 1831, he resigned from the army the following year to return to Ohio, where he worked as a civil engineer. He maintained his military interests, however, joining the Ohio Militia.

When the Mexican War broke out in 1846 Curtis was the adjutant general of Ohio's militia with the rank of colonel. After the state had sent two regiments into the field he accepted command of the 3rd Ohio Volunteers, which was mustered into service in June 1846 and mustered out a year later. It was during the Mexican War that Curtis, despite his West Point education, developed a strong dislike for regular army soldiers and their attitude towards volunteers. He wrote that he was "more mortified than indignant at the unnecessary desire manifested by the regular officers to put regulars forward and make them certain to be the authors of every acceptable movement." Even so he tried to get a regular commission as the war was winding down, but nothing came of his efforts, and he was mustered out with the rest of his volunteers.

On his regiment's discharge he moved to Iowa, where he opened a law office and became the mayor of Keokuk. In 1856 he was elected to the first of his three terms in the US House of Representatives. In 1861 he joined the Union army as colonel of the 2nd Iowa Infantry, and was appointed a brigadier-general of volunteers ranking from 17 May 1861. Accepting this commission, he resigned from Congress and was

Samuel Ryan Curtis. An acquaintance described him as "tall, finely though heavily formed, with high forehead, large hazel eyes, decidedly grave face... in demeanor serious, deliberate in speech and action undemonstrative." *(Military Images)*

assigned to duty at Frémont's headquarters to supervise military activities in and around St Louis. There he served well with fellow volunteers. Brigadier-General Franz Sigel, who saw service in Germany before coming to the United States but never served in the US regular army, recalled: "Before we reached Lebanon I was doubtful about my personal relations to General Curtis, which had been somewhat troubled by his sudden appearance at Rola and the differences in regard to our relative rank and position, but the fairness he showed in the assignment of the commands before we left Lebanon, and his frankness and courtesy toward me, dispelled all apprehensions on my part… ."

Curtis was given command of the Union army in Arkansas, holding on there to defeat Confederate Maj.Gen. Earl Van Dorn at the battle of Pea Ridge (7–8 March 1862). As a result he was named a major-general on 21 March, and shortly afterwards was given command of the Department of Missouri. There, however, he disagreed with Governor William Gamble, to the point that in May 1863 he was moved to command the Department of Kansas. From there he was moved further to command the Department of the Northwest. In August 1865, Curtis was named a US Peace Commissioner to negotiate treaties with various Plains Indian tribes, and three months later he was appointed to a commission to study the building of the Union Pacific Railroad, which was being laid down west from Omaha, Nebraska. While doing this work he died at Council Bluffs, Iowa, on 26 December 1866. He is buried in Oakland Cemetery, Keokuk.

DAVIS, Jefferson Columbus (1828–79)

Jefferson C.Davis (**see Plate D3**) was born in Indiana on 2 March 1828, and served in the 3rd Indiana Infantry during the Mexican War (1846–48), taking part in the battle of Buena Vista. Obviously a good soldier, he managed to obtain a direct commission as a second lieutenant in the 1st Artillery Regiment on 17 June 1848; in 1852 he was promoted to first lieutenant, and in 1861 to captain. He served in Fort Sumter's garrison during the bombardment, and was thereafter given command of the 22nd Indiana Volunteers by the state's governor Oliver Norton, a personal friend.

Since his family had moved to Kentucky when he was quite young, Davis' loyalty was at first in question – indeed, many Union soldiers mistrusted him to the end. James Connolly called him a "copperhead" – a pro-Southern Northerner – in a letter home written in December 1864. Sherman's staff officer George W.Nichols recalled, "It was said at the beginning of the war that General Davis had a leaning of strong sympathy toward the Rebels." He did not go South, however, and soon proved his loyalty to the army and administration in Washington. In December 1861 Davis was commissioned a brigadier-general of

Jefferson C.Davis, in a woodcut made from a photograph for *Harper's Weekly*.

volunteers. He commanded a division at the battle of Pea Ridge (7–8 March 1862) and again at Corinth (3–4 October).

Davis is most famous, however, for shooting his superior officer, Maj.Gen. William Nelson – a man who was almost universally disliked – in the lobby of the Galt House hotel in Louisville, Kentucky, on 29 September 1862. According to the account published in *Harper's Weekly*, Nelson, who had previously threatened to arrest Davis for not knowing the exact number of troops in his command, struck Davis twice in the face with the back of his hand after Davis demanded an apology. Nelson then turned and strode off into the ladies' parlor, saying, "Did you hear that damned rascal insult me?" Davis also left, but returned with a borrowed pistol. Nelson came out of the parlor just as Davis entered the hotel lobby, and Davis shot Nelson in the chest; he died some 15 minutes later.

Sherman pretty much summed up the feelings of the army top brass in a letter to his wife: "What a sad thing was Nelson's fate. I knew him well. He was a clever fellow, but very overbearing & blustering. Davis on the contrary was a modest bashful quiet but brave man. I cannot justify the act, but do not condemn it." Again Davis was aided by his powerful friend Governor Norton. Although he was arrested immediately, not only was he not prosecuted for the murder, but he was restored to duty only a few days after the shooting.

Davis served as a divisional commander at Murfreesboro (Stones River, 31 December 1862–3 January 1863), Chickamauga (19–20 September 1863), and in the drive to Atlanta. There he received command of XIV Corps, which he led in the March to the Sea and the Carolinas campaign (November 1864–March 1865). Nevertheless, his

An impression published in *Harper's Weekly* of the episode which was Davis' main claim to fame, when he shot and mortally wounded his superior, Gen.William Nelson, in the lobby of the Galt House hotel at Louisville, Kentucky. That Davis was not prosecuted for murder speaks volumes for Nelson's unpopularity.

promotion to major-general was by brevet, not as a regular officer. Many of his own soldiers opposed his promotion, citing – among other things – his bad treatment of local African-Americans during the March to the Sea (November–December 1864). After the war Davis was named a colonel in command of the 23rd Infantry. He served in Alaska and in the Modoc War, dying in Chicago on 30 November 1879. He is buried in the Crown Hill Cemetery, Indianapolis.

FRÉMONT, John Charles (1813–90)

John C.Frémont (**see Plate A2**) was born in Savannah, Georgia, on 21 January 1813. He attended Charleston College for two years, being expelled in 1831. Even so, he gained an appointment as teacher of mathematics on the USS *Natchez*, and subsequently as a lieutenant in the US Army Corps of Topographical Engineers in 1838. He had some political influence with Andrew Jackson's presidential administration, which eased his way into these positions. He was soon sent on a mapping expedition to western Minnesota, where he met Senator Thomas Hart Benton and fell in love with the senator's daughter Jessie. Despite strong objections from the senator, the couple wed in 1841. Thereafter Frémont led several mapping expeditions throughout the American West.

Frémont first gained fame in the Mexican War (1846–48), commanding the Battalion of California Volunteers as a major from July 1846 until discharged on 19 April 1847. However, he quarreled with the US Navy commander in California, which led to a court-martial; found guilty of mutiny and insubordination, Frémont resigned from the army in 1848. He remained in California, and bought land in Mariposa where gold was later found, making him well-to-do. Well known in the state, he used his position to run successfully for the US Senate in 1850 on the entry of California into the Union as a state. Frémont became one of the leaders of the new Republican Party and was its first candidate for president in 1856. In the final count he lost to Democrat James Buchanan by only 500,000 votes out of 21,000,000 votes cast.

When the war broke out he was appointed a major-general in the regular US Army and given command of the Department of the West. Although Frémont was popular with the press, he was less highly regarded by his soldiers. E.F.Ware, 1st Iowa Infantry, later wrote: "If there ever was an empty, spread-eagle, show-off, horn-tooting general, it was Frémont. I have no time here to go into the story of his eccentricities and follies, but we all despised him forever and forever more. He had no abilities of any kind… . He was weak and vain, and with a heavy touch of what 'Orpheus C.Kerr' called the 'damphool.'"

One of Frémont's misjudgements was his tendency to surround himself with special 'body-guards' in elaborate uniforms, who looked more

John Charles Frémont as he first appeared in Western garb in the pages of *Harper's Weekly*. John Pope wrote of him: "My first impressions of him were that he was a handsome and graceful man, short and slender, with black eyes and black curly hair, rather of the 'ringlet style.'"

like an opera army than a fighting force. The visiting French Army Lt.Col. Camille Ferri Pisani noted that Frémont's headquarters in St Louis, in one of the city's most beautiful houses, had "a military luxury and a display of military authority unknown in the United States and suggesting at once both a commander in chief and a proconsul."

Frémont also fell out of favor with the government in Washington. In August 1861 he issued a proclamation that had not been approved in advance by President Lincoln, declaring that civilians found under arms would be court-martialled and shot if convicted, and that slaves owned by those who aided the rebellion would be emancipated instantly. Lincoln, who feared offending slave-owners in border slave states such as Kentucky, was appalled. He quickly wrote to Frémont that his proclamation put Union military prisoners in danger, and moreover, that the emancipation clause "will alarm our Southern friends, and turn them against us… ." He asked Frémont to amend the proclamation accordingly. Frémont felt insulted, and his wife went East to explain Frémont's views to the president. Despite this lobbying, Lincoln ordered Frémont "to conform to, and not transcend" government policy.

Frémont, left, pictured in more conventional dress with his fellow Western general Nathaniel P.Banks in the 31 August 1861 issue of *Harper's Weekly*. A French observer, Lt.Col.Pisani, wrote that Frémont was "a man about fifty years old, average height, very thin and nervous. Obviously he is made of iron and accustomed to physical fatigue. His face, surrounded by graying hair and beard, is thin, dark, and tired, yet full of vivacity and intelligence. The fiery glance of two extremely deep black eyes lightens his face."

Frémont also ran into trouble with Missouri's governor, who took his complaints to Washington; with his fellow general Francis P.Blair and his family; and even with his own subordinates. Tales of corruption and fraud in his department began to reach Washington, and Lincoln finally wrote, "He is losing the confidence of the men near him, whose support any man in his position has to have to be successful." Frémont was relieved from command on 2 November 1861; never again given a command, he finally resigned from the army on 4 June 1864.

After his resignation he was nominated by radical Republicans and some "war Democrats" to stand for president against Lincoln in 1864, but was talked out of running. Eventually losing his California estates, Frémont lived largely on income from his wife's literary work. He was territorial governor of Arizona from 1878 until 1887, and was also restored to the army's list as a retired major-general. He died in New York City on 13 July 1890, and is buried in Rockland Cemetery, Piermont-on-the-Hudson, New York.

His fellow officer John Pope met Frémont in 1845, and later described him: "He talked very little and appeared to be as reserved in character as he was frugal in words." Pope later served with him in the early days of the war in the West, and noted: "General Fremont's unusual reticence and the extreme difficulty of seeing him, much less talking with him, was a great misfortune to him and I have no doubt led to much of his trouble and disappointment. His staff officers, who naturally were supposed to reflect his wishes and to express his orders, almost completely shut him off from the highest officers of his command by denying them admittance to his presence, or by so obstructing and delaying

Ulysses S.Grant as a major-general. Horace Porter, who joined Grant's staff in November 1863, described him as "a man of slim figure, slightly stooped, five feet eight inches in height, weighing only a hundred and thirty-five pounds, and of a modesty of mien and gentleness of manner which seemed to fit him more for the court than for the camp. His eyes were dark-gray, and were the most expressive of his features. Like nearly all men who speak little, he was a good listener; but his face gave little indication of his thoughts, and it was the expression of his eyes which furnished about the only response to the speaker... . His mouth, like Washington's, was of the letter-box shape, the contact of the lips forming a nearly horizontal line... . His hair and beard were of a chestnut-brown color. The beard was worn full, no part of the face being shaved, but, like the hair, was always kept closely and neatly trimmed... . His face was not perfectly symmetrical, the left eye being a very little lower than the right... . He never carried his body erect, and having no ear for music or rhythm, he never kept step to the airs played by the bands, no matter how vigorously the bass drums emphasized the accent... . In conversing he usually employed only two gestures; one was the stroking of his chin beard with his left hand; the other was the raising and lowering of his right hand, and resting it at intervals upon his knee or a table, the hand being held with the fingers close together and the knuckles bent, so that the back of the hand and fingers formed a right angle." *(Military Images)*

them, that many left without seeing him and in a most unfortunate state of feeling for future success."

GRANT, Ulysses Simpson (1822–85)

Hiram Ulysses Grant (**see Plate B2**), to use the name under which the general was baptized, was born on 27 April 1822 at Point Pleasant, Ohio, the grandson of a Revolutionary War soldier. He was appointed to West Point by his congressman, who registered him as Ulysses Simpson Grant, having forgotten his first name. At the time, Grant later wrote, "A military life had no charms for me… ." Grant was graduated 21st in the class of 1843, which also contained his future brother-in-law, Frederick T.Grant, who later served on his staff. Assigned to the 4th Infantry, in Mexico he received a brevet to first lieutenant for meritorious conduct at Molino Rel Rey (8 September 1847), and a brevet to captain for gallant conduct at Chapultepec (13 September). After the war he served as regimental quartermaster from September 1849 until he resigned from the US Army on 31 July 1854. Separated from his wife, who was possibly the single most important thing in his life, by his service in California, he began to drink more than he should have, and resigned rather than face the possible official consequences. His life thereafter until the Civil War was a series of failures, as a farmer, real estate salesman, and customhouse clerk. He finally took a job as a clerk in the leather store owned by two of his brothers.

When the Civil War broke out Grant wrote to the governor of Illinois offering his services, with hopes of getting a commission as brigadier-general of volunteers. Instead he was given command of a badly disciplined regiment, the 21st Illinois, as colonel. Whipping the regiment into shape, he received his brigadier-general's commission on 7 August 1861, due in part to the influence of an Illinois congressman, Elihu B.Washburne.

Grant took his new brigade to Belmont, Missouri, a Confederate outpost on the west bank of the Mississippi; here he made a successful if minor attack on 7 November 1861 that blooded his troops. He then commanded the army forces that took Forts Henry and Donelson (February 1862), being nicknamed "Unconditional Surrender" Grant from the terms he offered Donelson's commander. Grant's victories were bright spots in a dark year for the Union, and he was commissioned major-general of volunteers.

On 6–7 April 1862 Grant narrowly escaped a severe defeat at Shiloh at the hands of A.S.Johnson; he was loudly criticized, and Halleck took over his forces and led them to Cairo, with Grant as a bad-tempered second-in-command ready to quit. In June 1862 Sherman, one of Grant's closest subordinates and friends, wrote to his wife that Grant "is not a brilliant man… but he is a good & brave soldier tried for years, is sober, very industrious, and as kind as a child."

Halleck was called East on his promotion to overall command in July 1862, leaving Grant at the head of the weak Army of the Tennessee. After frustrating maneuvers which culminated in a limited victory at Corinth (3–4 October 1862), Grant moved against the strategic Mississippi stronghold of Vicksburg. During the subsequent siege newspaper reporter Sylvanus Cadwallader, who covered Grant during the war for the *New York Herald*, had an opportunity to observe his personal courage: "He had gone into the cramped exposed redoubt to see how the work was progressing and noticing the reluctance with which the men could be brought to the open embrasure, deliberately clambered on top of the embankment in plain view of the sharpshooters, and directed the men in moving and placing the guns. The bullets zipped through the air by dozens, but strangely none of them touched his person or his clothing. He paid no attention to appeals or expostulations, acting as though they were not heard; and smoked quietly and serenely all the time, except when he removed his cigar to speak to the men at work."

In May 1863 Grant fought a dazzling campaign of maneuver against separate Confederate forces commanded by J.E. Johnston and John

Grant first appeared in the pages of *Frank Leslie's Illustrated Newspaper* on 18 March 1862, to mark his victory at Fort Donelson; he is depicted wearing the stiffened black "Hardee" dress hat with upturned brim. At that date he wore a full-length beard, though he later trimmed it back. The opposing Maj.Gen. Leonidas Polk, meeting Grant after the battle of Belmont, noted that Grant "looked rather sad… like a man who was not at ease and whose thoughts were not the most agreeable."

C.Pemberton, culminating in victory at Champion's Hill on the Big Black River (16 May). After several attempts and a long siege Vicksburg finally surrendered on 4 July 1863, cutting the Confederacy in half from north to south. Grant received a commission as major-general in the regular army and Union command in the West. In October 1863 he marched to besieged Chattanooga; under his leadership, with help from Hooker, Sherman, and Thomas, the siege was lifted and Braxton Bragg's Confederate army was routed in a two-day battle at Lookout Mountain and Missionary Ridge (24–25 November 1963). Grant was then named the first lieutenant-general in the US Army since George Washington, and was brought East to take overall command.

Grant chose to stay with Meade's Army of the Potomac, while sending other forces under Sherman against Georgia, Banks against Texas, Butler against Richmond, and Hunter into the Valley of Virginia. Under Grant's supervizion the Army of the Potomac, checked in the Wilderness (5–6 May 1864), did not retreat as it had done so many times before, but headed south around the right flank of Lee's Army of Northern Virginia, towards Richmond. Lee was forced to fight a running series of battles in May and June (Spotsylvania, Yellow Tavern, and Cold Harbor) that ended up in trenches in front of Petersburg, Virginia, south of Richmond. Grant's losses were heavy, but Lee's were equally so and more difficult to replace.

Not letting up even while in a siege situation, Grant continued to probe Lee's lines, especially on his right, finally forcing him out his fortifications. On 2 April 1865, Lee abandoned Richmond and headed west, planning to turn south and join his forces with the Confederate army in South Carolina. Grant moved his army equally quickly, cutting Lee off and forcing the surrender of the Army of Northern Virginia at Appomattox on 9 April 1865.

As the most important general of the Union army, it was no surprise that Grant was nominated for president and won in 1868. His two administrations were, however, marred by scandals involving administration officers, although Grant himself was never accused of any wrongdoing.

Grant, left, discusses the terms for the surrender of Vicksburg, Mississippi, with Confederate Lt.Gen. John C.Pemberton. According to the despatch that accompanied this sketch in *Harper's Weekly*: "At three o'clock this afternoon [3 July 1863] the meeting of General Grant and Pemberton took place near the rebel work Fort Hill. After a conference of some two hours, in the most quiet and courteous manner, the two officers parted with a handshake that seemed most friendly. Quietly seated upon the grassy slope near the rebel works, one could only look with the greatest interest upon the scene."

Traveling through Europe after his second term, he returned to New York and became involved in a brokerage firm, Grant & Ward; the company went bankrupt, and he became unable to support himself. Mark Twain, the famous writer, admired the articles Grant produced on the war for the *Century Magazine*, and convinced him to write his memoirs. This he did, while dying from throat cancer; anxious to provide for his family, he finished the book only weeks before his death on 23 July 1885. The book, one of the best-written American auto-biographies ever printed, successfully maintained his family after his death. Grant is buried in a mausoleum on Riverside Drive, New York City. Sylvanus Cadwallader left a number of observations about the general:

"Grant always exhibited marvelous self-control and was thereby enabled to control others.... He had been driven into avocations which, to him, were humiliating, to obtain a bare support for his family. His army habits of undue conviviality unfitted him for close application to any business pursuit and made him untrustworthy in the estimation of his father and brothers, and of his father-in-law, W. Dent.... There was a strong element of Scotch thrift developed, which he retained to the end of his life.... There was a vein of carelessness and indolence running through Gen. Grant's character plainly discernible to those who knew him intimately, which seemed at variance with his other qualities of mind.... He disliked the laborious details of office work, and would have been a very inefficient Adjutant General of the United States Army. It was not so much a lack of knowledge and ability in this direction, as lack of application. His plans for marches were clearly outlined to his Adjutant, and Chief-of-Staff; and every detail of each quite apt to be thereafter wholly left to them for execution.... I never heard an oath (or any substitute for one) escape his lips. He abominated 'smutty' stories and would not listen to them."

GRIERSON, Benjamin Henry (1826–1911)

Benjamin Grierson **(see Plate G2)** was born in Pittsburgh, Pennsylvania, on 8 July 1826. Educated at a school in Youngstown, Ohio, he then taught music at several mid-western towns; in 1856 he opened a school at Meredosia, Illinois.

Grierson was taken onto the staff of Brig.Gen. Benjamin Prentiss at the beginning of the Civil War, but soon became major of the 6th Illinois Cavalry in October 1861. He was promoted to command of the regiment as colonel in April 1862.

Given command of detachments of his own regiment as well as men of the 7th Illinois Cavalry and 2nd Iowa Cavalry, totaling some 1,700 troopers, Grierson started off on 17 April 1863 from La Grange, Tennessee, on a 17-day-long raid through Alabama and Mississippi. His troops managed to avoid many of the units sent after them, although they fought a number of skirmishes on their way as they destroyed sections of two railroads and vast amounts of supplies. His cavalrymen finally arrived at Baton Rouge, Louisiana, on 2 May, at the end of the first long-range expedition Federal forces had made into Confederate territory.[1] The raid had proved that, in the words of Sherman, "the Confederacy was a hollow shell." Grant reported to Halleck that Grierson "had spread excitement throughout the state, destroying railroads, trestleworks, bridges, burning locomotives and railway stock, taking prisoners, and destroying stores of all kinds. To use the expression of my informant, 'Grierson has knocked the heart out of the State.'"

For this feat Grierson was made a brigadier-general of volunteers to date from 3 June 1863, and given command of the cavalry of XVI Corps. Grierson would have found that satisfying, as he was a great self-promoter, making sure that testimonials of his ability found their way into the public eye. He also tried to get other Union generals to plead his case for promotion; Sherman replied to such a request in February 1863, that he would "at once send you a letter to the Secy. of War, but cannot promise it will be of any value. I certainly wish your promotion if you want it."

Grierson spent 1864 and 1865 in the Army of the Mississippi as a cavalry division commander as well as commander of the army's cavalry corps from time to time, until relieved of duty by James Wilson, Sherman's new cavalry commander, who was junior in rank to Grierson. Going further West, he was involved in the taking of Mobile, Alabama, towards the war's end. After the war he

Benjamin Grierson depicted in *Harper's Weekly* in full cavalier style, the face taken from a photograph.

---

1 In 1959 the raid was used as the basis for a highly fictionalized motion picture, John Ford's *The Horse Soldiers*, starring John Wayne and William Holden.

was commissioned a major-general of volunteers on 19 March 1866, before being mustered out of the volunteer service on 30 April. He was commissioned directly into the regular army as colonel of the 10th Cavalry, an African-American regiment. Breveted brigadier-general and major-general for his service in the Southwest, Grierson was promoted to brigadier-general on 5 April 1890, and retired that July. He died at his summer home in Omena, Michigan, on 1 September 1911.

HALLECK, Henry Wagner (1815–72)

Henry W.Halleck (see Plate B3) was born at Westernville, New York, on 16 January 1815. Disliking the farming life which seemed to be his lot, he ran away and was taken care of by his maternal grandfather, who sent him to Hudson Academy and then Union College, where he was elected to Phi Beta Kappa. Known as "Old Brains," Halleck was graduated third in the West Point class of 1839, behind Isaac Ingalls Stevens – who was graduated with top honors and died at the battle of Chantilly in 1862 – and the second-place graduate, who died at sea in 1843. Halleck served as an assistant professor at the Academy while still an undergraduate there. After graduation he was assigned to the Corps of Engineers, working on New York coastal defenses before being sent to France to inspect French fortifications.

Halleck gained a reputation for his intellectual abilities with his publication *Bitumen and its Uses* (1841), and his appointment as a lecturer on military science and art by the Lowell Institute in Boston in 1845. His lectures at Lowell were published as *Elements of Military Art and Science*, which became a standard work among the armed forces of the period. In the Mexican War, while on his way to California, he translated Henri Jomini's *Vie Politique et Militaire de Napoleon*, which he published in 1864. He was breveted captain for meritorious services in California, where he served as the secretary of state. He was a member of the convention that formed the state's constitution, as well as chief-of-staff for lower California, and lieutenant-governor of Mazatlan, Mexico. He was named a captain in the Corps of Engineers in 1853 "for fourteen years of meritorious service."

Nevertheless, Halleck resigned his commission in August 1854; entering the bar, he became a partner in the law firm of Halleck, Billing, & Co in San Francisco. The following year he married a granddaughter of Alexander Hamilton. Offered a seat on the state supreme court, he declined it – as he did a chance at a US Senate seat. Instead he spent time in business and writing books on mining and international law, as well as serving in the California Militia.

Based on his reputation, on the outbreak of war Lincoln appointed Halleck a major-general in the regular army to rank from 19 August 1861, making him the fourth ranking general in the US Army. He was sent to St Louis in November 1861, to relieve Frémont. There he reorganized the National forces, which had been left in

Henry Halleck, an engineer, administrator, and author of several books, had more of the appearance of a bank teller than a soldier. John Pope later described him as "a black-browed saturnine man, heavy of figure and of feature… ." On 9 August 1862, *Harper's Weekly* reported: "Major-General Halleck, in personal appearance, is below the medium height, straight, active, and well-formed, and has a brisk energetic gait, significant of his firm and decisive character. His nose is delicate and well formed, his forehead ample, and his mouth by no means devoid of humour. His eye is of a hazel color, clear as a morning star, and of intense brilliancy… ." *(Military Images)*

Halleck was sometimes fancifully portrayed as a fierce battlefront soldier, as in this *Harper's Weekly* impression of 26 April 1862. Nevertheless, the 9 August issue of *Harper's* noted that "General Halleck in camp and in the field is hardly the same person who might have been seen quietly gliding from the Planters' House to head-quarters in St Louis. He does not look a whit more military in appearance, but looks, in his new and rich though plain uniform, as if he were in borrowed clothes. In truth, he bears a most striking resemblance to some oleaginous Methodist parson dressed in regimentals... ."

chaos by Frémont's administration. In overall command of the theater in which the Union finally scored victories such as Forts Henry and Donelson, Island No. 10, and Elkhorn Tavern, he gained a rather undeserved reputation as a field commander. In fact, when he actually took the field to replace Grant after Shiloh for the move on Corinth, he moved as slowly as McClellan did on the Peninsula against an equally outnumbered enemy. The Confederates were able to abandon Corinth and remove all their supplies safely as a result.

William T.Sherman, who had difficulties with Halleck during the war, wrote afterwards: "General Halleck was a man of great capacity, of large acquirements, and at the time [1862] possessed the confidence of the country, and of most of the army. I held him in high estimation, and gave him the credit for the combinations which had resulted in placing this magnificent army of a hundred thousand men, well equipped and provided, with a good base, at Corinth, from which he could move in any direction."

As a result of this reputation, however well deserved, Halleck was called to Washington in July 1862 to become the army's general-in-chief. Once there, he found himself directing George B.McClellan, who resented losing the office that Halleck assumed. McClellan wrote to his wife on 30 July: "I am sorry to say that I hear that too much faith must not be rested in Halleck – I hope it is not so – but will be very careful how far I trust him.... He has done me *no good yet.*" After Halleck ordered McClellan to abandon his position outside Richmond and march to the help of the Army of Virginia south of Washington, McClellan wrote, "I am forced to the conclusion that H. is very dull, very incompetent...." This opinion would not change so long as Halleck remained as McClellan's superior officer, or even after McClellan left the service. Despite the element of personal resentment, however, McClellan's estimation was correct: Halleck proved a failure in his new post. He involved himself in minute details of troops and matériel, while passing on to his subordinates the responsibilities for his own failure to oversee the overall war effort.

Despite his failings, Halleck remained in that position even when Grant was named a lieutenant-general and became the actual head of the army; thereafter Halleck was essentially reduced to the position of the army's chief clerk. John Pope, who admitted that it was difficult for anyone who served with Halleck to write about him without bias, later described him thus: "He seemed to proceed on the theory that everyone around him was seeking to get some advantage of him and he was con-tinually taking precautions against his officers, which did not attract their regard to him.... He had a large ability of the closet kind and was in no sense brilliant – with theories often sustained and put forth by the best authorities he was familiar; acts to illustrate these theories he was utterly incompetent to do. He considered that any statement or report that might, even for the time, be beneficial to the public was justifiable whether true or not and this theory he practiced to the injury of some of the officers who served under him and to the damage of his own character. He was an office man altogether and in matters of administration he had both ability and industry."

After the war Halleck was given command of the Military Division of the James until August 1865, when he returned to San Francisco in command of the Pacific Division. He was sent to Louisville, Kentucky, in 1869 as commander of the Division of the South. He died there on 9 January 1872, and is buried in Green-Wood Cemetery, Brooklyn, New York.

HOWARD, Oliver Otis (1830–1909)

Oliver O.Howard (see Plate E1) was born at Leeds, Maine, on 8 November 1830. After graduating from Bowdoin College in Maine he attended the US Military Academy; he was graduated fourth in the class of 1854 – the first place being achieved by Robert E.Lee's son G.W.Custis Lee. Assigned to the Ordnance Corps, he spend half his pre-war career as an assistant professor of mathematics at West Point, and the rest on Ordnance Corps business.

Despite his lack of command experience, 1st Lieutenant Howard was commissioned colonel of the 3rd Maine Infantry in May 1861. He resigned his regular commission on 7 June as he moved up in rank. He commanded a brigade at First Manassas (Bull Run, 21 July 1861), and was commissioned a brigadier-general of volunteers to date from 3 September. Howard commanded a brigade in II Corps during the Peninsula campaign, where he lost his right arm during the battle of Seven Pines (Fair Oaks, 31 May–1 June 1862). Returning to duty after recuperating, he commanded the rearguard in the retreat from Second Manassas (29–30 August), and the Second Division, II Corps at Antietam (17 September).

Commissioned a major-general of volunteers on 29 November 1862, Howard was given command of XI Corps in time for Fredericksburg (13 December). He commanded this corps, made up in large part of European immigrants, at Chancellorsville (1–6 May 1863). There, holding the right of the Union Army, he disregarded warnings of Confederates approaching his right flank and failed to post sufficient pickets or alert his subordinates to the possibility of attack. It was a fatal error: "Stonewall" Jackson's troops smashed into his position and totally routed the corps, and only nightfall and Jackson's mortal wounding saved his corps from destruction. The popular blame was assigned to the foreign rank and file rather than to Howard, whose reputation survived this blunder.

Oliver Otis Howard as a major-general, after he had stopped shaving his upper lip. Frank Haskell described him in 1863: "Howard is medium in size, has nothing marked about him, is the youngest of them all [Army of the Potomac corps commanders], I think – has lost an arm in the war, has straight brown hair and beard, shaves his short upper lip, over which his nose slants down, dim blue eyes, and on the whole, appears a very pleasant, affable, well dressed little gentleman." (Military Images)

Again, at Gettysburg, Howard led XI Corps into battle on 1 July 1863 – some of the first Union infantry on the field – but they fought badly, and his corps was essentially out of action after that first day. Despite this, Howard received the thanks of Congress for his selection of Cemetery Hill and Cemetery Ridge as a fall-back position after Federal forces had been driven out of the town.

Howard's corps had lost all credibility among the other troops of the Army of the Potomac after Chancellorsville and Gettysburg. In the fall of 1863, XI Corps and the understrength XII Corps were sent west to help break the siege of Chattanooga. There Howard served well enough to be assigned command of IV Corps in the drive to Atlanta. On the death of James McPherson, Sherman gave him command of the Army of the Tennessee; this force, comprising XV and XVII Corps, made up the right wing for the March through the Carolinas. In 1864 Sherman wrote to Halleck, "Howard is a Christian, elegant gentleman, and conscientious soldier. In him I made no mistake."

Sherman's artillery chief, Thomas Osborn, wrote of Howard: "General Howard's ability as a soldier is almost eclipsed by his kindness and consideration for his troops, their comfort and welfare in every particular, his persistent fighting when engaged, and determination to win; the reckless disregard of his own person; his implicit obedience to all authorized orders, and the child-like simplicity of his social character. He has in his personal address a nervous and unstudied gesture, which to people unacquainted with him, appears feminine. Still his address is elegant and his language indicates a mind of very superior cultivation.

"His most marked characteristic is his especial military ability and unerring judgment in military operations. His energy of character I have never seen surpassed, and with all he is the highest toned gentleman I have ever known. It appears impossible for him ever to think amiss. He is by no means the profound thinker and learned man that General Sherman is, nor has he his large natural ability. He does not call out from his troops the enthusiastic applause that Generals Logan and Hooker do; yet every officer and man has an unbounded confidence in him, and never question that an order from him is from the highest known authority, or even to think of going beyond it for a superior decision. I have never been in an Army where such implicit confidence was displayed in its leader."

Another of Sherman's staff officers, George W.Nichols, wrote: "General Howard is a man whose religious convictions are intense, positive, entering into the coloring of every event of his life. When exposed to fire, there is no braver man living than he. He does not go into action in the Cromwellian spirit, singing psalms and uttering prayers, but with a cool and quiet determination which is inspired by a lofty sense of a sacred duty to be performed. His courage is a realization of the strength of a spiritual religion rather than a physical qualification. The General is constantly censured for rashly exposing himself to the fire of the enemy...."

After the war Howard returned to the regular army as a brigadier-general. Deeply religious, he took up the cause of the African-American and, as a result, was named first commissioner of the Bureau of Freedmen, Refugees, and Abandoned Lands in May 1865. This organization was created to help African-American former slaves adjust to free life. It was, however, largely to fail; despite Howard's personal honesty and desire for progress – supported by many of those who came into the organization – the Bureau as a whole was riddled with corruption. Howard went in front of a court of inquiry in 1874, but was exonerated.

Howard was a co-founder of Howard University in Washington, DC, one of the primary African-American places of higher learning, and was a director of an African-American bank. He also saw service as superintendent of West Point, and in the West. He was promoted to major-general in 1886 and commanded the Division of the East until he retired in 1894. He then made his home in Burlington, Vermont, taking time to help set up Lincoln Memorial University at Harrogate, Tennessee. He died in Burlington on 26 October 1909, and is buried in Lake View Cemetery there.

KILPATRICK, Hugh Judson (1836–81)

Hugh Kilpatrick (**see Plate G3**) was born near Deckertown, New Jersey, on 14 January 1836. Although he was poorly educated he was accepted into West Point, where he dropped the name Hugh, going by Judson Kilpatrick (although he was also known as "Little Kil"). He was graduated 17th in the class of May 1861, a year in which the 1861 graduating class was sent out into the world a month early because of the war, while what would have been the class of 1862 was actually graduated in June 1861. One of his classmates was Orville Babcock, who would serve as an aide-de-camp to Grant from 1864.

Immediately after graduation Kilpatrick accepted a commission as captain in the 5th New Jersey Infantry, with which he was wounded at Big Bethel, Virginia (10 June 1861), in the war's first action of any note. In September 1861 he transferred to become the lieutenant-colonel of the 2nd New York Cavalry, being promoted colonel of that regiment in December 1862. He was commissioned a brigadier-general of volunteers on 14 June 1863, commanding a brigade and later a division of cavalry in the Army of the Potomac.

Kilpatrick was sent West in April 1864 to command a division in Sherman's army. Badly wounded at Resaca (15 May 1864) at the beginning of the Atlanta campaign, he returned to duty in July 1864. Thereafter he served in cavalry battles around Atlanta, gaining the nickname "Kil-Cavalry" for his constant hard driving that wore out his command's horses.

Although almost a teetotaller who declined to play cards, Kilpatrick was, however, a notorious rake who usually had women of questionable morals around his headquarters. He was also vain and boastful. Major James Connolly wrote home: "Kilpatrick is one of the most vain, conceited, egotistical little popinjays I ever saw. He has one redeeming quality – he rarely drinks spirituous liquors, and never to excess. He is a very

Hugh Judson Kilpatrick as a major-general. George W.Nichols wrote of him: "In personal appearance [he] is of slight stature, but broad-chested and wiry-limbed. His face is expressive of determination and daring. A firm chin, earnest mouth, prominent nose, clear gray eyes, and expansive forehead, make up a striking physiognomy. His beard is reduced to side-whiskers... . In conversation he speaks earnestly and rapidly... ." (*Military Images*)

Judson Kilpatrick liked to surround himself with women. Here he stands in a doorway between two ladies, in the uniform of a brigadier-general with the buttons set in pairs. *(Military Images)*

ungraceful rider, looking more like a monkey than a man on horseback." Even so, when Sherman began his March to the Sea in November 1864 he picked Kilpatrick to command his cavalry, saying, "I know that Kilpatrick is a hell of a damned fool, but I want just that sort of man to command my cavalry in this expedition."

Connolly had a chance to observe Kilpatrick closely. On one occasion, he wrote, "Kilpatrick came out in his bare head and shirt sleeves to the fire in front of our tents this evening and regaled us with an anecdotal history of his student days at West Point. He told us many anecdotes of our General McCook and the rebel, General Wheeler." Major Thomas Osborn, the artillery commander of the Army of the Tennessee, wrote home in February 1865: "I consider [Confederate cavalry commander Joseph] Wheeler and Kilpatrick officers of about the same calibre, neither of them large. General Howard has recommended that if a Cavalry Corps is organized for this Army, that it be given to General Mower. I think this would be a great improvement on the present. Kilpatrick would command a division well enough under a superior, but he is barely fit to command himself."

Successful in both the March to the Sea and the March through the Carolinas in winter 1864–65, Kilpatrick ended the war with a brevet as a regular major-general as well as a commission as major-general of volunteers awarded on 19 June 1865. After the war he was named minister to Chile, serving until 1868. He returned to run for Congress, unsuccessfully, and was reappointed to Chile in 1881. He died there, in

Santiago, on 4 December 1881, aged not quite 46;
his body was returned to be buried at West Point.

LOGAN, John Alexander (1826–86)

John A.Logan (see Plate H2) was born in Jackson
County, Illinois, on 9 February 1826. With only a
patchy education, he served from June 1847 to
October 1848 as a second lieutenant in the 1st
Additional Illinois Volunteers, although he saw
no combat during the Mexican War. A Democrat,
he later sat in the Illinois legislature and, in 1858,
was elected to Congress as strongly pro-slavery. He
supported Stephen Douglas in the 1860 election,
but spoke out strongly for the Union after
southern states began to declare themselves independent, even though his brother-in-law accepted
a Confederate commission. He joined a Michigan
unit as a volunteer in time for First Manassas
(Bull Run, 21 July 1861), but then returned to
southern Illinois to recruit the 31st Illinois, to
which regiment he was named commander.

Present in November 1861 at Belmont, where
he attracted Grant's attention when his horse was
killed, Logan was wounded at Fort Donelson the
following February. For his services he was named
a brigadier-general of volunteers to rank from 21
March 1862, receiving command of a brigade

John Alexander Logan. Staff
officer George W.Nichols
noted: "Nor is any one likely
to forget the General's personal
appearance who has ever had
an opportunity of seeing him.
That lithe, active figure; that
finely-cut face, with its heavy
black mustache overhanging
a sensitive mouth; that black
piercing eye, that open brow,
shaded by the long black hair –
all make up a striking figure."
(Military Images)

and later a division in the Army of the Tennessee. A highly successful
commander despite his lack of professional training, Logan was
promoted to major-general on 13 March 1863, and given command of
the Third Division in XVII Corps, commanded by James McPherson.

Logan led the attack when the mine was exploded in the siege of
Vicksburg, and went on to command XV Corps in the Atlanta campaign.
He was wounded again at Dallas, Georgia, during this campaign (25 May
1864). On the death of James McPherson he assumed command of the
Army of the Tennessee, but Sherman gave permanent command of the
army to Oliver Howard. As Sherman later wrote, "I did not consider him
to the command of three corps. Between him and General Blair there
existed a natural rivalry. Both were men of great courage and talent, but
were politicians by nature and experience, and it may be that for this
reason they were mistrusted by regular officers like Generals Schofield,
Thomas, and myself." (Logan was deeply hurt by this, and after the war
wrote *The Volunteer Soldier in America* to prove that volunteers made better
soldiers than professionals.) Logan left his command temporarily to
campaign for pro-war candidates in Illinois during the 1864 elections,
but returned to lead XV Corps from Savannah through the Carolinas.

Grant later wrote that he judged Logan as competent a divisional
commander as could be found in or out of the army and equal to higher
command. George W.Nichols called Logan "a firm friend, a good hater,
and an open fighter...." Horace Porter recalled "his swarthy features
and long, coal-black hair giving him the air of a native Indian chief" –
hence his nickname, "Black Jack."

John A. Logan – fifth from right – photographed with his staff in Vicksburg after the city's fall. Logan wears the regulation double-breasted frock coat with two rows of eight buttons set in pairs, a tall black hat – probably a stripped "Hardee" – light-colored gauntlets and tall boots of soft leather. *(Military Images)*

John Pope described Logan thus: "His swarthy countenance, his fierce black eyes and long black hair, his erect martial figure and impetuous mien were all known to all the armies with which he served and the representative bodies which he adorned. Everyone, however, did not know the tenderness of his heart and the nobility of his soul. Free from envy or jealousy, he entered into whatever work was before him with perfect sincerity and with all his might. His animated face and his waving sword were seen in the front of every battle in which he was engaged, and his bold bearing and cheerful words brought encouragement and courage wherever they were seen on the line of battle."

After the war Logan returned to politics, serving both as a Representative and Senator from Illinois as well as organizing veterans' societies, and was an unsuccessful candidate for vice-president in 1884. He died as a senator on 26 December 1886, and is buried in the Soldiers' Home National Cemetery.

McCLERNAND, John Alexander (1812–90)

John A. McClernand **(see Plate A3)** was born near Hardinsburg, Kentucky, on 30 May 1812. Self-educated, he was admitted to the bar in 1832 and went into politics, serving in both the Illinois legislature and US Congress. His sole military experience before the Civil War was a stint as a private in the Illinois Militia during the Black Hawk War for three months in 1832.

Grant later wrote of McClernand: "General McClernand was a politician of very considerable prominence in his State; he was a member of Congress when the secession war broke out; he belonged to that political party which furnished all the opposition there was to a vigorous prosecution of the war for saving the Union; there was no delay in his declaring himself for the Union at all hazards, and there was no uncertain sound in his declaration of where he stood in the contest before the country. He also gave up his seat in Congress to take the field in defence of the principles he had proclaimed."

As a reward for his political stance in sensitive southern Illinois, McClernand was commissioned brigadier-general of volunteers to date from 17 May 1861, and promoted to major-general dating from 21 March 1862. Despite his unattractive qualities, in fact his military record was not as bad as is suggested in the memoirs left by some professional soldiers. He gave good service at Belmont and Forts Donelson and Henry. Although his planned expedition against Vicksburg in October 1862 failed, he then turned to capture Arkansas Post in January 1863. Placed under Grant's command, he commanded XIII Corps during the siege of Vicksburg that spring.

Vain, selfish, and pompous, McClernand fought his war with an eye to the media. He issued vainglorious statements for the press after every action, victorious or not. Western professional soldiers loathed him, which made the conduct of co-ordinated operations very difficult. Sherman wrote in January 1863, "To me McClernand is one of the most objectionable [Union generals] because his master is Illinois and personal notoriety...." He would later write, "McClernand is an old politician who looks to self aggrandizement, and is not scrupulous of the means," adding still later, "McClernand is a dirty dog, consumed by a burning desire for personal renown." Indeed, according to Sherman, McClernand "shew[ed] the white feather at Shiloh...."

Grant also disliked McClernand, finding him "highly insubordinate." On 17 January 1863, Grant visited McClernand's headquarters: "It was here made evident to me that both the army and navy were so distrustful of McClernand's fitness to command that, while they would do all they could to insure success, this distrust was an element of weakness." Finally, after McClernand issued a statement to the press calling his men "the heroes of the campaign" after a disastrous attack on the Vicksburg lines, Grant relieved him.

McClernand was considered important enough by the Lincoln administration to be returned to duty as commander of XIII Corps in February 1864, when he served in the Red River campaign to the further damage of his reputation. Finally, falling ill, he resigned from the army on 30 November 1864. Returning to the Illinois state capital of Springfield, McClernand campaigned against Lincoln's re-election. He continued in Democratic politics until his death in Springfield on 20 September 1890. He is buried there.

McPHERSON, James Birdseye (1828–64)

James B. McPherson (**see Plate D2**) was born near Clyde, Ohio, on 14 November 1828. His blacksmith father, mentally unstable, was largely unable to support the family, so McPherson had to go to work at a young age. The owner of a local store where he found employment befriended the boy and made sure he received an education at the Norwalk Academy in Ohio. The merchant then got McPherson into West Point, where he was graduated first in the class of 1853,

ahead of John Schofield, Philip Sheridan, Benjamin Franklin Smith, and John Bell Hood.

Appointed into the Corps of Engineers by virtue of his success, McPherson spent his pre-war career working on fortifications on both coasts, including those on Alcatraz Island in San Francisco Bay. When the war broke out he was named to Halleck's staff as an aide-de-camp; he subsequently joined Grant's staff, serving in 1862 as chief engineer during the capture of Forts Henry and Donelson, the battle of Shiloh, and the move on Corinth. He also spent some time as superintendent of railroads in West Tennessee.

McPherson was strongly recommended for advancement by both Grant and Halleck – one of the few things upon which they did agree – and was commissioned brigadier-general of volunteers on 19 August 1862. Two months later he was promoted to major-general, and in January 1863 he was assigned command of XVII Corps under Grant.

Western troops, used to informal discipline, did not like regular army officers, but some made an exemption – Lucius Barber of the 15th Illinois wrote: "When [McPherson] assumed command of the division, the boys were nearly all prejudiced against him as they were against all West Point graduates, but when we learned the many noble qualities that he possessed, our dislike changed into esteem and later, when we saw his matchless skill as a military leader, and above all, his great kindness to his soldiers to whose appeals for justice he never turned a deaf ear, our esteem amounted to almost veneration, and soon McPherson's name became synonymous with all that was good and noble – a perfect gentleman in every respect and every inch a soldier."

For his service in the Vicksburg campaign McPherson was named a brigadier-general in the regular army to date from 1 August 1863. He was given command of the Army of the Tennessee on 26 March 1864, and led it in the Atlanta campaign. Sherman sent McPherson to strike the rear of the retreating Confederate army at Snake Creek Gap, but his maneuvers there seemed too cautious for Sherman's taste, as the Confederates escaped. Even so, Sherman used McPherson's forces repeatedly to attack Confederate positions during the advance on Atlanta. While on this campaign McPherson became engaged to a woman from Baltimore and applied for leave to marry her, but Sherman, feeling that his presence was too important to be spared, refused this request.

On 22 July 1864, when the Confederates were attacking Sherman's positions around Atlanta in desperation, McPherson personally reconnoitered the lines. He and his staff came into a small clearing already occupied by a company from the 5th Confederate Regiment, which opened fire on the mounted party, and McPherson was killed. The Confederate company commander, Capt. Richard Beard, would write: "Even as he lay there, dressed in his Major General's uniform, his face in the dust, he was as magnificent a looking picture of manhood as I ever saw." Sherman was later reported as saying: "The army and

James Birdseye McPherson, whose great promise was cut short in battle at the age of 35 years. After a difficult childhood he was graduated first in his class at West Point; appointed to the Engineers, as was usual for the Academy's star cadets, he nevertheless showed great gifts as a field commander – which was not so usual. Brigadier-General Willard Warner later wrote that McPherson "had such noble beauty of form and countenance, such winning gentleness of expression and manner; his face, which in repose had an expression of almost womanly sweetness, would so light up and blaze with fiercest courage and daring in the moment of battle, that in danger he was worshipped as a hero; in quiet regarded in tenderest love as a man...." (Military Images)

country have sustained a great loss by the loss of McPherson. I had expected him to finish the war. Grant and I are likely to be killed, or set aside after some failure to meet popular expectation, and McPherson would have come into chief command at the right time to end the war. He had no enemies."

McPherson's body was returned to Ohio and buried near where he played as a boy.

ORD, Edward Otho Cresap (1818–83)

Edward O.C.Ord **(see Plate D1)** was born in Cumberland, Maryland, on 18 October 1818, and was raised in Washington. He was graduated from West Point 17th in the class of 1839, below Halleck but above the future Army of the Potomac artillery commander Henry Hunt. He was commissioned in the 3rd Artillery, and his first service was in Florida. In the Mexican War (1846–48) he was assigned to the garrison at Monterey, California. Thereafter he was on duty in the Pacific Northwest, being promoted captain in 1850. In 1859 he took part in the expedition that captured John Brown and put down his abortive slave rebellion at Harper's Ferry, Virginia. Back in California when the Civil War broke out, he was appointed a brigadier-general of volunteers on 14 September 1861, and ordered back East.

There were doubts that Ord might be too pro-slavery to fight well for the Union. He wrote to Sherman about these concerns: "There is no doubt of it, I was in 49 & until 54, a pro slavery man, and I am not quite such a radical now as to think we can turn all those black people loose

among the whites, any more than we could so many tame Indians, with advantage to either race." Nonetheless, he was given command of a brigade in the defenses of Washington, seeing action at Dranesville. On 3 May 1862 he was appointed a major-general and sent to the Western theater.

Ord missed the battle of Iuka (19–20 September 1862) because of an acoustical fluke that caused him not to hear gunfire within several miles of him, but he performed well in attacking Earl Van Dorn's retreating Confederates several days later. Ord was wounded in this action and unable to return to duty until June 1863, when he was named to replace McClernand in command of XIII Corps. The corps was sent to southern Louisiana after the surrender of Vicksburg. Ord was then transferred to command of XVIII Corps, part of the Army of the James, serving both in the Shenandoah Valley and in the attack upon the works around Richmond. There, in the capture of Fort Harrison on 29 September 1864, Ord was again badly wounded. Although he was not able to return to duty until January 1865 he was then given command of the Army of the James (replacing Benjamin Butler), along with command of the Department of North Carolina. Ord stayed with Grant's army, finishing the war at Appomattox.

After the war Ord became a brigadier-general in the regular army dating from 26 July 1866, serving in a number of posts before his retirement in 1881. On a ship bound from New York to Cuba in 1883 he came down with yellow fever, and died in Havana on 22 July. His body was returned to the United States, and he is buried in Arlington National Cemetery.

Peter Joseph Osterhaus, remembered mainly for being a German officer forced to flee his homeland in the aftermath of the failed liberal uprisings of 1848. He fought throughout the war, rising from major to major-general of volunteers, and holding temporary command of a corps under Sherman. *(Military Images)*

OSTERHAUS, Peter Joseph (1823–1905)

Peter Osterhaus **(see Plate F1)** was born in Coblenz, Germany, on 4 January 1823. He was trained as an officer in the Prussian Army, but was one of those forced to flee after the failure of the liberal revolutions of 1848. Osterhaus came to the USA; after a period living in Illinois and working as a clerk he finally settled among the large German population of St Louis.

Osterhaus was commissioned major of a pro-Union Missouri battalion, and served in that capacity at Wilson's Creek in August 1861. After his unit was mustered out of service he became colonel of the 12th Missouri Infantry in December 1861. He was commissioned brigadier-general of volunteers and commanded a division at the battle of Pea Ridge (7–8 March 1862). He also held a divisional command in the Vicksburg campaign, being wounded at Big Black River in May 1863. Returning to duty, Osterhaus served with that part of the Union army at Chattanooga that completely routed the Confederates on the southern end of Missionary Ridge (25 November

(continued on page 103)

1: Brigadier-General Samuel Curtis
2: Major-General John Frémont
3: Major-General John McClernand

A

1: Major-General Nathaniel Banks   2: Lieutenant-General Ulysses S.Grant
3: Major-General Henry Halleck

LEFT TO RIGHT **1: Major-General William Rosecrans 2: Major-General Don Carlos Buell 3: Major-General Edward Canby**

C

1: Major-General Edward Ord
2: Major-General
   James McPherson
3: Major-General
   Jefferson C.Davis

D

LEFT TO RIGHT 1: Major-General Oliver Howard 2: Major General William T.Sherman 3: Major-General Henry Slocum

E

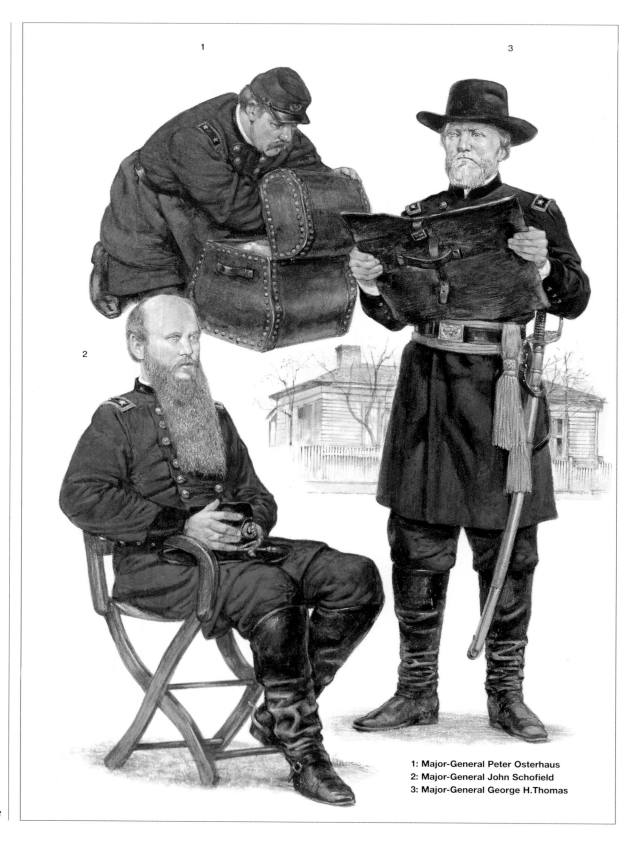

1: Major-General Peter Osterhaus
2: Major-General John Schofield
3: Major-General George H.Thomas

F

1: Brigadier-General James Wilson   2: Colonel Benjamin Grierson   3: Brigadier-General Judson Kilpatrick

G

LEFT TO RIGHT   **1: Major-General Alpheus Williams   2: Major-General John Logan   3: Major-General Francis Blair**

1863). He was promoted to major-general on 23 July 1864 after further service in the Atlanta campaign. During the March to the Sea and then the March through the Carolinas (November 1864–March 1865) he had occasion to command XV Corps.

After the war Osterhaus returned to St Louis where he operated a wholesale hardware business. He also spent time in France, where he represented the USA as consul in Lyons, and served as a consul in Germany. He was placed on the regular army list as a retired brigadier-general on 17 March 1905, and died at Duisburg, Germany, on 2 January 1917. He is buried in Coblenz.

ROSECRANS, William Starke (1819–98)

William S. Rosecrans (**see Plate C1**) was born in Delaware County, Ohio, on 6 September 1819. At the age of 18 he was appointed to West Point through a direct application to the secretary of war, and was graduated fifth in the class of 1842, which also included many of the Confederacy's future generals such as George Washington Rains, D.H. Hill, Richard H. Anderson, Lafayette McLaws and James Longstreet, as well as the Union Army's John Pope. Rosecrans was nicknamed "Old Rosy" at West Point, a nickname which followed him throughout his life.

Married in 1843 to a native New Yorker, he was assigned to be assistant professor of engineering and natural philosophy at West Point, where he served for four years. He was then sent to oversee engineering works at various places along the east coast. He resigned his commission in 1853 and became a civil engineer and architect in Cincinnati, Ohio. Two years later he became superintendent of a coal company in Coal River, western Virginia, but left to go into the coal oil business in Cincinnati in 1857.

When the war broke out Rosecrans joined McClellan's staff as the chief engineer and aide-de-camp. On 21 June 1861 he was commissioned colonel of the 23rd Ohio, receiving his commission of brigadier-general four days later. He then commanded a brigade in McClellan's western Virginia campaign, where his name attracted public notice.

Rosecrans had a way of winning the trust of the common soldier. Constantin Grebner, a soldier in the 9th Ohio, recalled that when Rosecrans assumed command of his brigade he visited each company, "addressing to each a kind word and a quip, sometimes clever, sometimes not, but always apposite to the unit at hand.... General Rosecrans soon enjoyed increased trust with every last man of the corps." Major James Connolly wrote home in July 1863, "with Rosecrans to lead we think we can go anywhere in the confederacy."

He tended to get excited and stammer when in action. *New York Herald* correspondent William Shanks reported, "I have known him, when merely directing an

William Rosecrans was pictured when commanding troops in western Virginia. The September 1861 issue of *Harper's Weekly* included this description: "Socially the General unites to the refinement of the gentleman the frank, free-spoken manner so taking among our Western population. In person he is little above the middle height, rather thin, and very erect, with no feature so striking as his broad forehead and clear gray eyes." Although a schoolmasterly intellectual rather than a veteran line officer, "Old Rosy" was very popular with his troops. *(Military Images)*

orderly to carry a dispatch from one point to another, grow so excited, vehement, and incoherent as to utterly confound the messenger. In great danger as in small things, this nervousness incapacitated him from the intelligible direction of his officers or effective execution of his plans."

General Jacob Cox, who shared a tent with Rosecrans in West Virginia in 1861, wrote: "His impulsiveness was plain to all who approached him; his irritation quickly flashed out in words when he was crossed, and his social geniality would show itself in smiles and in almost caressing gestures when he was pleased. In discussing military questions he made free use of his theoretical knowledge, often quoted authorities and cited maxims of war, and compared the problem before him to analogous cases in military history. This did not go far enough to be pedantic and was full of lively intelligence; yet it did not impress me as that highest form of military insight and knowledge which solves the question before it upon its own merits, through a power of judgment and perception ripened and broadened by the mastery of principles which have ruled the great campaigns of the world. He was fond of conviviality, loved to banter good-humoredly with his staff officers and intimates, and was altogether an attractive and companionable man, with intellectual activity enough to make his society stimulating and full of lively discussion."

After West Virginia, Rosecrans was given command of the left wing of the Army of the Mississippi in the campaign that took Corinth after Shiloh. When Pope went East, Rosecrans took over his command, being named a major-general of volunteers from 21 March 1862. He did not distinguish himself in the battles of Iuka and Corinth (September and October 1862), where his laxity frustrated Grant's plans for a double envelopment of Van Dorn's forces. He was sent to relieve Don Carlos Buell in Kentucky, this command now being named the Army of the Cumberland.

After fighting off Braxton Bragg at Murfreesboro (Stones River, 31 December 1862 – 3 January 1863), he fell back to a line along the Duck River. In June 1863, Rosecrans began a campaign of maneuver that ended up with his troops taking Chattanooga bloodlessly (7 September). The Confederates struck back at Chickamauga (19–20 September), battering the Union army: James Longstreet exploited a gap which Rosecrans' deployments had created in the Union center, and the day was saved largely by Geoge H.Thomas' hard-fought defense. Nevertheless Rosecrans ended up besieged by Bragg in Chattanooga, with only a rugged mountain trail for resupply. Grant was sent to relieve him in October 1863.

Sherman compared the two generals: "Rosecrans may be Grant's superior in intellect, but not in sagacity, purity of character and singleness of purpose. Rosecrans is selfish & vainglorious. Grant not a bit so." Rosecrans left to

An impression of Rosecrans from *Harper's Weekly* when he was appointed commander of the Army of the Ohio. General Jacob Cox, his tentmate in West Virginia in 1861, wrote: "His general appearance was attractive. He was tall but not heavy, with the rather long head and countenance that is sometimes called Norman. His aquiline nose and bright eyes gave him an incisive expression, increased by rapid utterance in his speech, which was apt to grow hurried, almost to stammering, when he was excited."

command the Department of Missouri in 1864. His time after the war was spent largely on leave, awaiting orders; he finally resigned his regular army commission on 28 March 1867.

Newspaper correspondent Whitlaw Reid wrote that Rosecrans was "easy of access, utterly destitute of pretence, and thoroughly democratic in his ways. With his staff his manner was familiar and almost paternal; with private soldiers always kindly. In the field he was capable of immense labor; he seemed never to grow weary, and never to need sleep. Few officers have been more popular with their commands, or have inspired more confidence in the rank and file."

Brigadier-General John Beatty of his command recalled: "Rosecrans is of medium height and stout.... Rosecrans indulges in an oath now and then; but is a member of the Catholic Church in good standing.... Rosecrans is an educated officer, who has rubbed much against the world and has experience.... Rosecrans' laugh is not one of the free, open, hearty kind...." Beatty was another observer of Rosecrans' knack for making himself popular with his enlisted men: "On review, the other day, he saw a sergeant who had no haversack; calling the attention of the boys to it he said: 'This sergeant is without a haversack; he depends on you for food; don't give him a bite; let him starve.'" On the other hand, Sherman felt that Rosecrans surrounded himself "with a set of flunkeys… pouring the oil of flattery that was sickening to all true men."

In 1868 Rosecrans became minister to Mexico, but he was removed from that office by President Grant a year later. He then retired to a ranch near Redondo Beach, California. He was elected to Congress from there, becoming chairman on military affairs and serving until 1885. From then until 1893 he was registrar of the Treasury. He died at his California ranch on 11 March 1898. Originally buried in Rosedale Cemetery, Los Angeles, his body was re-interred in Arlington National Cemetery in 1902.

SCHOFIELD, John McAllister (1831–1906)

John M.Schofield (see Plate F2) was born at Gerry, New York, on 29 September 1831, but taken as a youth to Illinois. He worked as a surveyor and a school teacher in Wisconsin before accepting an appointment to West Point, where he was graduated seventh in the class of 1853. After service in Florida he was appointed professor of physics at Washington University, St Louis, while on leave from the Army. On the outbreak of the war he was named mustering officer for Missouri.

As a major in the 1st Missouri Infantry, Schofield served on Nathaniel Lyon's staff at Wilson's Creek in August 1861. He was named brigadier-general of volunteers on 21 November, and given command of Missouri's Union militia. He led this force, formed as the Army of the

John M.Schofield. In the words of George W.Nichols, "At the first view of his round and well-developed head, his resolute mouth, and calm, reflective eyes, one is impressed with the idea that he is in the presence of a statesman rather than a soldier... ." At first Schofield did not demonstrate enough dash to gain Sherman's approval; but he entrusted this sober commander with the defence of Tennessee when he set off on his March to the Sea, and Schofield performed well during John Bell Hood's attempt on Nashville. (Military Images)

Frontier, from October 1862 until April 1863. He was named a major-general in November 1862, but was not confirmed by the Senate until he was appointed again on 12 May 1863. At that time Schofield was in command of a division of XIV Corps in Tennessee. From May 1863 until January 1864 he commanded the Department of the Missouri. In 1864 Sherman wrote to Halleck, "Schofield is also slow and leaves too much to others...."

However, during Sherman's March to the Sea in November–December 1864, Schofield was given command of the Army of the Ohio – also known as XXIII Corps – which was left to defend Tennessee. He maneuvered skilfully in the face of the Confederate advance on Nashville, and at Franklin (30 November) his troops repulsed John Bell Hood's head-on assaults with heavy loss, before withdrawing to Nashville. There his command took part in George H.Thomas' attack that essentially destroyed Hood's army. Thereafter Schofield was sent to North Carolina; here his forces made a separate advance from the coast to capture Wilmington on 22 February 1865, and then fanned out to take New Berne, Kinston, and Goldsboro before the war ended.

Brigadier-General Willard Warner later recalled, "General Schofield, though less widely known than either Sherman or Thomas, yet had the entire confidence and perfect respect of his own army, and of all who were competent to judge him, as a soldier of skill and courage, and as a pure patriot and just man."

George W.Nichols wrote: "General Schofield is a gentleman of fine address and elegant manners. There is nothing of the plausible sycophant either in his words or his actions. He listens well, talks but little, and appears to reflect and carefully weigh both what he hears and says... General Schofield not only possesses will and purpose, but he is perfectly versed in that technical knowledge of his profession without which will is almost valueless. While he may not be gifted with that dash and spirit which characterize other commanders, he has a calm assurance and a sober judgment which are never disturbed, even in the hour of repulse or disaster, and which is quick to seize the moment when success, wrung from doubt, carries victory."

After the war Schofield went to Texas to negotiate France's withdrawal from Mexico. He was named secretary of war in 1868, but soon resigned and served as superintendent of West Point from 1876 until 1881. He became general-in-chief of the Army in 1888, and retired in September 1895. He died in St Augustine, Florida, on 4 March 1906, and is buried in Arlington National Cemetery.

SHERMAN, William Tecumseh (1820–91)

Tecumseh Sherman (see Plate E2) – his baptismal name, given in honor of the famous Shawnee chief, though he had no Native American blood – was born in Lancaster, Ohio, on 8 February 1820, one of eleven children of a lawyer. His father died in 1829, and the boy was sent to be raised by Thomas Ewing, a US senator – whose daughter he would later marry, and whose wife had him rebaptized William.

A woodcut of Schofield from *Harper's Weekly* catches his calm and deliberate character.

William T.Sherman, in a *Harper's Weekly* woodcut made from a photograph. George Ward Nichols of his staff later wrote: "In person General Sherman is nearly six feet in height, with a wiry, muscular, and not ungraceful frame. His age is only forty-seven years, but his face is furrowed with deep lines, indicating care and profound thought.... His eyes are of a dark-brown color, and sharp and quick in expression. His forehead is broad and fair, sloping gently at the top of the head, which is covered with thick and light-brown hair, closely trimmed. His beard and moustache, of a sandy hue, are also closely cut."

Ewing secured him a place at West Point, where he was graduated sixth in the class of 1840, along with George H.Thomas and Richard S.Ewell. Commissioned into the 3rd Artillery, Sherman was named acting adjutant general of the Department of California in May 1847. He served there until 1849, when he was named an aide-de-camp to Major-General P.F.Smith and acting adjutant general of the Pacific Division, which was headquartered at San Francisco. In 1850 he was made a captain and appointed commissary of subsistence in California. He resigned his commission in 1853, to take a post with a San Francisco bank.

When the Civil War broke out, Sherman was superintendent of the Louisiana State Seminary of Learning and Military Academy; he resigned this post when the state seceded. That May he wrote his brother, "Really I do not conceive myself qualified for Quarter Master General, or Major General." Returning to take a commission as colonel of the 13th US Infantry, he fought at First Manassas (Bull Run, 21 July 1861). He was named a brigadier-general of volunteers on 7 August, although five months later he again wrote to his brother, "I do not feel confident at all in Volunteers." He was sent to Kentucky, but his expressed opinion that it would take 200,000 men to put down the rebellion gave his peers the idea that he had become mentally unstable. These press reports led to a mistrust of the media that would last his lifetime. He was relieved by Don Carlos Buell, and was sent to join Halleck in St Louis. He commanded a division at Shiloh (6–7 April 1862), for which he was made a major-general ranking from 1 May. At this time he also developed a close working relationship with Grant.

In December 1862 Sherman led an unsuccessful drive on Chickasaw Bluffs north of Vicksburg; but he was given command of XV Corps in 1863, leading it during Grant's campaign

Sherman after having taken Atlanta, photogaphed on his horse Duke within the Confederate defenses of the city. *(Military Images)*

against that fortress which ended with its surrender that July. He then went with Grant to break up the siege of Chattanooga. As his troops were preparing, Sherman accompanied his family, who were staying with him, onto a river steamer; the family would go to Ohio, while Sherman would get off at Memphis. On board, Sherman noticed that his son Willy, who had been with him in San Francisco, was missing. A regular army officer found the boy and brought him on board, but soon Willy developed typhoid fever. The child died, and Sherman, who had remained in his marriage for the sake of his children, was devastated, blaming himself for the boy's death. Sherman wrote to his wife that October, "Why should I ever have taken them to that dread climate? It nearly kills me to think of it. Why was I not killed at Vicksburg and left Willy to grow up to care for you?"

After the battle of Lookout Mountain at Chattanooga (24 November 1863), Grant left the trusted "Cump" Sherman in charge of the Western theater when he went East to assume overall command of the Union armies, despite Sherman's delicate emotional condition. With overall command of George H. Thomas' Army of the Cumberland, James B. McPherson's Army of the Tennessee, and John M. Schofield's Army of the Ohio – some 100,000 men in all – Sherman fought a war of maneuver all the way to Atlanta, which he took (1 September 1864) after John B. Hood, given command of the city, had spent his forces in assaults. After chasing Hood's army west of Atlanta, Sherman convinced

Grant to let him march through Georgia to the Atlantic Ocean. This March to the Sea reached Savannah by 21 December, having inflicted great damage at minimal cost. Then he turned northward through the Carolinas, finally accepting the Confederate surrender near Durham, North Carolina.

Sherman was blunt in his speech. General John Geary wrote home that once, in Savannah, he attended church, and a priest asked his permission regarding a detail of the service: "After some 'heming and hawing,' the Clergyman said, well Genl, the diocess [sic] of Georgia requires us to pray for certain persons. Will that be objectionable, to which the Gen replied, yes, certainly, pray for Jeff Davis. Pray for Jeff Davis? Certainly pray for the Devil too. I don't know any two that require prayers more than they do, pray for them certainly."

Fellow general John Pope wrote of Sherman: "He is perhaps the most original and interesting talker in this country and has apparently inexhaustible stores of knowledge and experience on almost every subject to draw upon. It is not so much what he recounts as what he suggests that makes his conversation so entertaining and instructive." Staff officer George W.Nichols agreed: "General Sherman's memory is marvelous. The simplest incidents of friendly intercourse, the details of his campaigns, citations of events, dates, names, faces, remain fresh in his mind.... He is also remarkably observant, especially of the conduct and character of the officers of the army.... When the responsibilities of the hour are cast aside – and he throws them off with the utmost facility – he enters into the spirit of a merry-making with all the zest and appreciation of the jolliest of the party. He has a keen sense of wit and humor, and not infrequently he is the centre and life of the occasion.... He converses freely, yet he is reticent to the last degree, knowing how to keep his own counsel, and never betraying his purposes. He is cautious, and often suspicious.... His unmeasured scorn and contempt are visited upon pretense, spurious philanthropy, arrogance, self-conceit, or boasting....

"His constitution is iron.... In the field he retires early, but at midnight he may be found pacing in front of his tent, or sitting by the camp-fire smoking a cigar.... He falls asleep as easily and quickly as a little child – by the roadside, upon the wet ground, on the hard floor, or when a battle rages near him.... He has a keen sense of the beauty of nature, and never is happier than when his camp is pitched in some forest of lofty pines, where the wind sings through the tree-tops in melodious measure, and the feet are buried in the soft carpeting of spindles. He is the last one to complain when the table fare is reduced to beef and 'hard tack'...."

Newspaper correspondent Sylvanus Cadwallader later wrote of Sherman: "As a corps and department commander, Sherman had no superior when all the then circumstances and environments were taken into account. He was pre-eminently a man of action, and exhibited his greatest qualities in aggressive movements and campaigns. The impetuosity of his character was exemplified whenever he was in supreme command....

"He was never subjected to the test of a defensive campaign; but it is not probable that he could have equaled Gen. Joseph E.Johnston, had their positions been reversed. He would have chafed like a caged wild beast, would have rushed into hopeless battle, would have risked too much upon the decision of one day's fighting. He was thoroughly subordinate and obedient to higher military authority, and enforced his favorite maxim, that 'the first duty of a soldier was obedience,' by obeying all orders in letter and spirit. This quality, perhaps above all others, endeared him to Gen. Grant. But he lacked Grant's superb equipoise. He often failed to control his temper."

In 1866 Sherman was named commander-in-chief of the army. He placed his headquarters in St Louis in 1874, disliking Washington politics. He retired on 8 February 1884, and moved to New York, where he died on 14 February 1891. He is buried in Cavalry Cemetery, St Louis.

SLOCUM, Henry Warner (1827–94)

Henry W.Slocum (see Plate E3) was born at Delphi, New York, on 24 September 1827. He attended Cavenovia Seminary, thereafter teaching school until he was appointed to West Point. He was graduated seventh in the class of 1852, and saw service in the South until his resignation in 1856 to practice law. Returning to New York, he moved to Syracuse where he became county treasurer and was elected to the state legislature. He remained in touch with the military, serving as an instructor in the New York State Militia with the rank of colonel.

Slocum was named colonel of the 27th New York Infantry on 21 May 1861, and fought at First Manassas (Bull Run, 21 July 1861), where he was wounded. After recovering he was made a brigadier-general of volunteers and given command of a brigade in VI Corps. He soon became a divisional commander and was named major-general on 25 July 1862. He commanded the division throughout the Peninsula campaign, Second Manassas, and Antietam (June, August, and September 1862). Thereafter he was given command of XII Corps, which did not see service at Fredericksburg but was badly battered at Chancellorsville (1–6 May 1863). His corps held the extreme right flank of the Union army at Gettysburg (1–3 July 1863).

Both XI and XII Corps were sent West to serve at Chattanooga under Joseph Hooker's command. Slocum, being senior to Hooker, protested at this and sent in a letter of resignation. This was refused, but he was given an independent command defending the Nashville & Chattanooga Railroad. From there he was sent to command the District of Vicksburg.

When McPherson was killed in July 1864, Howard took over the Army of the Tennessee, while Slocum was brought back to command XX Corps. For Sherman's March to the Sea through Georgia in winter 1864, Slocum was commander of XIV and XX Corps which made up Sherman's left wing – designated the Army of Georgia. Slocum had his detractors during the subsequent March through the Carolinas. Just outside Columbia, in February 1865, Thomas Osborne wrote home, "Slocum is doing nothing. The feeling of disgust toward him in this

Henry Warner Slocum. Staff officer George Nichols wrote: "His personal appearance is prepossessing. Long, wavy brown hair, brushed back behind his ears, sparkling brown eyes, a heavy brown mustache, a height above the medium, and a manner which inspired faith and confidence, make up a most attractive figure." Not much liked as a personality, and attracting differing opinions as to his military talents, Slocum performed well at Bentonville in March 1865 when the left flank of Sherman's armies, guarded by Slocum's two-corps Army of Georgia, was surprised by J.E.Johnston's Confederate command. *(Military Images)*

Army [of the Tennessee] is giving way to bitterness. General Blair, who is a very prudent man, in speaking of officers, comments severely on him this P.M."

Then came the battle of Bentonville (19–20 March 1865), when the Union left was suddenly attacked by J.E.Johnston's Confederates. Slocum was a major player in this action, and Osborne changed his tune, writing home: "This battle has placed Slocum firm on the record and has now all to his support. It was his first great battle, and he fought it well. Since leaving Columbia he has more than ever shown a spirit of cordial co-operation and support. He acknowledges to General Blair, his chagrin at not having himself taken Columbia, and said he owed his failure to do so to his inability to bring the XIV A.C. up in time. I have always since Gettysburg had a strong prejudice against him. His peculiarities are unpleasant, and one is not apt to reform his prejudices in favor of an unpleasant man. He did well here, and I am glad of it."

Slocum resigned his commission on 28 September 1865. Returning to New York, after turning down a regular army colonel's commission, he moved to Brooklyn from where he was sent to the House of Representatives for three terms (1869–1873, 1883–1885). He died in Brooklyn on 14 April 1894, and is buried in Green-Wood Cemetery.

THOMAS, George Henry (1816–70)

George H.Thomas (see Plate F3) was born in Southampton County, Virginia, on 31 July 1816. Appointed to West Point, he was graduated 12th in the class of 1840. He was assigned to the 3rd Artillery, and saw action against the Seminoles and in the Mexican War (1846–48). He was breveted captain for gallant conduct at Monterey, and major for gallant and meritorious conduct at Buena Vista. In 1850 he was sent to West Point as instructor of artillery and cavalry. He received promotion to captain in 1853, but in 1855 was transferred to the 2nd Cavalry as a major. While serving with that regiment he was wounded in a skirmish on the Clear Fork of the Brazos River in August 1860.

When the Civil War began, Thomas broke with his family to stay loyal to the Union, despite an offer from Virginia's governor to become the state chief of ordnance (he and his sisters never spoke again). Thomas was promoted to colonel and given command of a brigade that served in the Shenandoah Valley during the First Manassas campaign (July 1861). One of the few from that command to be noticed, he was promoted brigadier-general of volunteers on 17 August and was sent to Kentucky to serve under Don Carlos Buell. There he won a decisive defensive battle at Mill Springs (19–20 January 1862); and then fought at Shiloh (6–7 April) in the Army of the Ohio. Thomas was promoted to major-general of volunteers ranking from 25 April, and went on to serve as a divisional commander at the siege of Corinth, at Perryville (8 October), and Murfreesboro (Stones River, 31 December 1862–3 January 1863).

Thomas' shining moment came at Chickamauga on 19 September 1863, when he stubbornly held a position at Horseshoe Ridge on the Union left while around him other Federal troops, including the overall commander William Rosecrans, fled back towards Chattanooga. Gaining the nickname "The Rock of Chickamauga," Thomas was rewarded with the rank of brigadier-general in the regular army on 27

October. Rosecrans' army was besieged in Chattanooga when Grant arrived to exercise overall command of the Western theater. He ordered Hooker's two corps, which included Thomas' troops, to attack Confederate positions at Missionary Ridge (24 November 1863). Thomas' men were sent against a line of rifle pits at the bottom of the slopes; but once there they found their overlooked position untenable, and they pressed on up through the Confederate lines on the slopes to take the mountaintop itself, in what became known as "the battle above the clouds."

Thomas was given command of the Army of the Cumberland, which served in the Atlanta campaign. When Sherman got permission to cut loose and march through Georgia, he detached Thomas' command to defend Nashville. "I have again and again tried to impress on Thomas that we must assail & not defend," Sherman complained to Grant in June 1864, adding, "Thomas has a Head Quarter Camp in the Style of Halleck at Corinth. Every aid, & orderly with a wall tent and a Baggage train big enough for a Division. He promised to send it all back but the truth is every body there is allowed to do as he pleases...."

After being thrown back with terrible casualties at Franklin (30 November 1864) by John Schofield, John Bell Hood's Army of Tennessee besieged Thomas' troops in Nashville. Grant pressured Thomas to attack, but he waited for better weather, taking advantage of the time to better equip and organize his largely inexperienced troops. Finally, one step ahead of Grant's determination to go to Nashville and personally remove Thomas from command, he struck Hood's forces on 15 December, turning first his left and then both flanks in two days of fighting that saw the Army of Tennessee virtually destroyed – the only example of a large Civil War army being eliminated as the result of a single battle. After this triumph Thomas was also known as "The Sledge[hammer] of Nashville." Again, this resulted in his promotion, to major-general in the regular army.

One of his staff officers, Horace Porter, later wrote, "'Old Pap Thomas,' as we all loved to call him, was more of a father than a commander to the younger officers who served under his immediate command, and he possessed their warmest affections." Thomas was popular with all ranks; James Connolly wrote home after McPherson's death, "That is a severe loss, but his place can be filled; should we lose old father Thomas though, it would hurt us equal to the loss of an entire Division."

John Pope met Thomas during the fighting around Monterrey, Mexico, in 1846: "He was, as always, tall and stalwart, but in those days he had not put on the flesh which rather disfigured him in later years." Summing him up, Pope concluded, "He was great in defensive operations, and in no case was he ever driven from any position he

George H. Thomas, the hero of Chickamauga, Lookout Mountain and Nashville, whose loyalty to the Union cost him his family in Virginia. Major James Connolly described him when they arrived outside Atlanta as standing "like a noble old Roman, calm, soldierly, dignified; no trace of excitement about that old soldier who had ruled the storm at Chickamauga." *(Military Images)*

occupied. His mind seemed to work slowly, but the results of his deliberate thought were always sound, and what is more to the purpose as illustrating his character, he always maintained them with a persistency that might sometimes be called obstinacy.... I presume he had the natural ambition of the soldier who occupies high place and command in a great war, but if he did have it, he certainly never betrayed it to his closest observers.... He was utterly without arrogance or ostentation and easily approachable by persons of all ranks. His manner, while undemonstrative, was kind and considerate and when his troops began to know him they began to feel that confidence in his judgment and affection for his person which finally became an unreasonable passion which scarcely permitted criticism of anything he did or said."

Sylvanus Cadwallader, a newspaper correspondent at Grant's headquarters, later wrote that Grant lacked confidence in Thomas: "This was not so much a distrust of his soldierly qualifications and reliability in defensive operation, as fear that when he was left to act on his own responsibility he would be too slow in assuming the offensive. I think this estimate of Gen. Thomas will be considered just by future historians. He was unquestionably one of the greatest subordinate commanders the war produced, but he never distinguished himself unqualifiedly in any independent command." In this, of course, Cadwallader overlooks his destruction of Hood's Army of Tennessee at Nashville.

This was, however, the general opinion of Thomas. Sherman wrote to Halleck in 1864, "George Thomas, you know, is slow, but as true as

Thomas resting in the field during a campaign with his Army of the Cumberland; his troops adored this fatherly figure, and called him "Old Pap Thomas". Grant grew frustrated with his slow and deliberate preparations at Nashville, but when Thomas was finally ready for battle on 15 December 1864 he smashed John Bell Hood's Army of Tennessee in one of the most complete victories of the whole war. *(Battles and Leaders of the Civil War)*

steel..."; he later wrote that Thomas' characteristics were "steadiness, good order, and deliberation – nothing hasty or rash, but always safe, 'slow, and sure.'" Grant to Sherman on 21 January 1865: "He is possessed of excellent judgment, great coolness and honesty, but he is not good on a pursuit." His own soldiers often called him "Old Slow Trot."

Thomas remained in command of the Department of the Tennessee until 1867. For political reasons President Andrew Johnson wanted him to replace Grant as the Army's general-in-chief, but Thomas refused, and in 1869 was given command of the Division of the Pacific. He died at his San Francisco headquarters on 28 March 1870; and is buried in his wife's hometown of Troy, New York.

WILLIAMS, Alpheus Starkey (1810–78)

Alpheus S.Williams (**see Plate H1**) was born at Saybrook, Connecticut, on 20 September 1810. He was graduated from Yale University in 1831 and then studied law. He spent much time in both domestic and international travel, returning to open a law office in Detroit; he was also named a probate judge and owned a newspaper. In December 1847 he was elected lieutenant-colonel of the 1st Michigan Volunteers. The regiment was sent to Mexico, where Williams gained valuable field experience, but by then the major battles were over and the unit saw no combat before being discharged in July 1848. Williams stayed active in state military affairs, and at the outbreak of the Civil War he was a brigadier-general of state volunteers, serving as president of the state military board.

Williams quickly received a commission as a US brigadier-general of volunteers on 9 August 1861, and commanded a brigade under Nathaniel P.Banks during "Stonewall" Jackson's Valley campaign, and at Cedar Mountain (9 August). Banks' command was enlarged and named XII Corps of the Army of the Potomac, subsequently seeing service at Antietam (17 September 1862). There the corps commander was killed and Williams assumed command for a short time, until replaced by a regular army officer, Henry Slocum. After Gettysburg (1–3 July 1863) XII Corps was sent to Chattanooga, and Williams was given a division in XX Corps in the Army of the Cumberland.

At times Williams found himself in command of the corps during the Atlanta campaign, the March to the Sea, and the March through the Carolinas in winter 1864–spring 1865, but he was always soon replaced by a regular army officer. He was breveted major-general in 1866. Major-General John W.Geary, a divisional commander in Sherman's army, wrote to his wife in April 1865 that Williams did not get the corps command because he "proved unsatisfactory to Gen Sherman. [William T.] Ward & Williams both drink too much, and neither could be trusted."

Alpheus Starkey Williams, whom George W.Nichols described as "heavily built, about the medium height, with a large beard and still larger mustache, which lends a peculiar expression to the face – an expression, however, which is forgotten when the genial, kindly eyes light up in conversation." His reputation as a heavy drinker was probably what kept Williams from a permanent corps command, but he actually led XX Corps for much of Sherman's final campaigns, and was more popular than the general he replaced, Henry Slocum. (*Military Images*)

However, Quartermaster William Le Duc noted that at the Grand Review in Washington after hostilities had ceased, "Williams, who had succeeded Slocum, was a great favorite with officers and men, and had ably commanded the Corps from Atlanta to North Carolina." George W.Nichols said of him, "A favorite with officers and men, he is delightfully hospitable, possesses an unfailing fund of good humor, is thoroughly subordinate, unenvious, unselfish, and as cool and self-possessed in the battle-field as at his quarters."

In 1866 Williams, out of the Army, was named minister to the Republic of Salvador, where he served until 1869. Returning to Michigan, he was elected to the House of Representatives in 1874 and 1876. He died while in Congress on 21 December 1878, and is buried in Elwood Cemetery, Detroit.

WILSON, James Harrison (1837–1925)

James H.Wilson (**see Plate G1**) – "Harry" to his friends – was born on 2 September 1837 at Shawneetown, Illinois. He first attended McKendree College in Illinois, but after a year switched to West Point. He was graduated sixth in the class of 1860, behind Horace Porter, one of Grant's senior aides, and before the future Confederate general Stephen D.Ramseur.

Assigned to the Corps of Topographical Engineers, Wilson spent most of the summer of 1861 recovering from cholera. After recovery he was picked as chief topographical engineer on the Port Royal expedition and then for the entire Department of the South. He joined George McClellan's staff for the Antietam campaign, and then moved to Grant's headquarters where he ended up as a lieutenant-colonel, serving as inspector general of the Army of the Tennessee and staff engineer; in this post he was reunited with an old friend, James McPherson. While there, he reported to Grant that his cavalry "were excellent material, but all untrained and badly deficient in discipline. In the advance they did well, but in the retreat they were entirely unmanageable…. The entire organization was lacking in coherence, co-operation, and steadiness." Grant was quite impressed by this confident young man, and on 30 October 1863 had him commissioned brigadier-general of volunteers, suggesting that he had "uncommon qualifications" for a cavalry command.

Wilson was thereafter a man marked out for advancement. Assistant Secretary of War Charles A.Dana noted in 1863, "His leading idea is the idea of duty, and he applies it vigorously and often impatiently to others. In consequence he is unpopular among all those who like to live with little work. But he has remarkable talents and uncommon executive powers, and will be heard from hereafter." Continuing as a staff engineer even in his new rank, Wilson was finally sent to be chief of the cavalry bureau in Washington. There he proved to be an outstanding administrator, cleaning up shady buying practices and beginning a program to make sure that every cavalry regiment was armed with repeating carbines. Then Grant brought him to the Army of the Potomac; and on 7 April 1864 he was given command of the Third Division, Cavalry Corps, under Philip Sheridan – much to the annoyance of several officers senior to him. One of these, George Custer, opined that Wilson was an "imbecile."

Never before having held a command of any size, Wilson faced a learning experience when the Cavalry Corps took the lead in the drive to Petersburg and then against Jubal Early's campaign in the Shenandoah Valley. His only independent action was a raid to break up the Richmond & Danville, Petersburg & Weldon, and Southside railroads south and west of Petersburg. After finishing this mission Wilson's division ran into a full infantry division supported by cavalry, and came close to being captured (Burke's Station & Ream's Station, 22–23 June 1864); he finally managed to escape, but with the loss of all his cannon, most of his wagons, and 900 men. One trooper of the 2nd Ohio later recalled that among the survivors, "Genl Wilson's name was a stench in their nostrils...."

Wilson continued in command, however, and his division was sent to the Shenandoah Valley, where it opened the successful battle of Opequon Creek (third battle of Winchester, 19 September 1864), and then fought again at Fisher's Hill (22 September). Grant then sent Wilson to the Military Division of the Mississippi to serve under Sherman. That commander later recalled: "General Grant, in designating General Wilson to command my cavalry, predicted that he would, by his personal activity, increase the effect of that arm 'fifty per cent,' and he advised that he should be sent south, to accomplish all that I proposed to do with the main army; but I had not so much faith in cavalry as he had, and preferred to adhere to my original intention of going myself with a complete force."

Wilson dismissed Sherman's cavalry chiefs, all of whom were superior to him on the regular army rank list, including George Stoneman and

James "Harry" Wilson, second right, photographed when a divisional commander in the Army of the Potomac's Cavalry Corps under Philip Sheridan, second left. Wilson wears sky-blue enlisted man's trousers, a waist-length single-breasted jacket, and a kepi with a dark band. This very plain outfit contrasts sharply with the fancy jacket and flowing shirt collar of Alfred T.A. Torbert, right, and the positively biblical appearance of David Gregg, left. *(Military Images)*

Benjamin Grierson. He formed their troops into the Cavalry Corps, Military Division of the Mississippi; and then organized, equipped, and drilled the cavalry that Judson Kilpatrick would later lead to the sea, while Wilson took command of another three-division cavalry corps in the Army of the Cumberland under George Thomas. At the battle of Nashville (15–16 December 1864) it was Wilson's troopers who swept up thousands of Hood's Confederate stragglers after their defeat.

After this action Wilson's men went into winter encampment; but times were hard, and supplies only reached his widely dispersed units slowly. On 29 January 1965, Wilson was greeted by cries of "Hard Tack! Hard Tack!" while riding through one of his camps. Never one to accept typical volunteer ideas of discipline, the young general made the men parade for eight hours in the cold to punish them. Another trooper, of the 27th Indiana Mounted Infantry, recalled: "General Wilson came to us from the army of the Potomac and brought with him much of the

Wilson – sitting on the second step with his leg drawn up – surrounded by his staff. Note their informality, and their mixture of regulation, non-regulation, and enlisted men's uniforms. *(Military Images)*

'grand review' style of that army; that of itself was enough to prejudice all Western soldiers against him, for if there was anything Western troopers did hate, it was anything that was done for mere style.… But added to this love of show, he seemed to study just how to keep every soldier in his whole army on duty every day… we had general orders from General Wilson read to us every morning, and upon almost every conceivable subject… just as though we had been in the service almost three years and yet did not know how to make ourselves comfortable and keep clean.… But after all was said and done, when we broke camp in the spring we were no better prepared for the campaign than when we went into camp." Wilson did, however, gain some approval by getting his troopers the latest Spencer repeating carbines to replace the odd assortment of inferior arms that they had previously carried.

In the spring of 1865, Wilson led his independent corps – more than 13,000 strong – in a raid designed to support Canby's campaign against Mobile, Alabama. He almost completely destroyed Nathan B.Forrest's command at Selma, Alabama (2 April), with his troopers assaulting the earthworks as infantry. Wilson then turned to raid through the South, destroying stores and factories, and riding without opposition through the streets of the Confederacy's first capital, Montgomery, Alabama. On 20 April he reached Macon, Georgia, where he learned that the Confederate armies under Robert E.Lee and Joseph Johnston had surrendered. Wilson's last raid was the most successful independent cavalry operation of the war; Confederate Maj.Gen. Richard Taylor noted that his "soldierly qualities are entitled to respect; for of all the Federal expeditions of which I have any knowledge, his was the best conducted." Moreover, at only 27, he was the youngest commander of an army in American military history.

Promoted a major-general of volunteers on 21 June 1865, Wilson reverted to the rank of lieutenant-colonel of the 35th US Infantry in 1866. Having clashed with the new President Andrew Johnson in Tennessee he was lucky to get even that; Johnson thought him only a "bumptious puppy." His actual service, however, was with the engineers. Wilson resigned in 1870 to move to Wilmington, Delaware, and entered the railroad business. In 1875 he had a falling-out with Grant as a result of the so-called "Whiskey Scandal" and the two refused to speak to each other again. Wilson visited China in 1885. In 1898, when war broke out with Spain over Cuba, Wilson – still only 61 – volunteered his services and was commissioned a major-general of volunteers. He saw service in Puerto Rico, and after hostilities ended was named military governor of Matanzas District, Cuba. While there his wife Ella was mortally injured when her clothing caught fire; Wilson then returned to the US and resigned his commission. He later returned to the service, however; and was named second in command of the American relief column that marched to Beijing during the Boxer Rebellion in 1900. In 1901 he was placed on the retired list of the Army as a brigadier-general. Wilson represented the United States at the coronation of King Edward VII in London in 1902. He died in Wilmington on 23 February 1925, and is buried in the Old Swedes Churchyard there. Only three other Union generals outlived him.

THE PLATES: WEST

According to regulations, general officers were distinguished by knee-length, double-breasted, dark blue frock coats, with two rows of eight gilt buttons set in pairs for brigadier-generals and two rows of nine buttons in threes for major-generals. Standing collars and 'jampot' cuffs were faced with dark blue velvet, and the cuffs bore three small buttons at the rear, two on the facing and one above it. Rank was indicated by gold-edged transverse shoulder straps of black or dark blue velvet, bearing a single silver five-pointed star for a brigadier-general and two stars for a major-general. Trousers were plain dark blue, and were worn either over or tucked into black boots – high spurred riding boots with soft flapped tops reaching above the knee were favored on campaign. The general officers' regulation buff silk waist sash, with tasseled ends knotted on the left side, was often omitted in the field; likewise the dress sword belt, of gold lace stripes on red leather, was normally replaced by a plain black belt, the rectangular gilt buckle plate bearing the arms of the USA – the spread eagle and motto within an open-topped wreath. The regulation staff and field grade officers' sword had a brass (or gilt) pommel, knuckle-bow and guard, black leather grips bound with copper wire, and a blued steel scabbard with (gilt) brass fittings.

In fact, loose 'sack' coats resembling the soldiers' jackets were sometimes preferred over the frock coat for wear in the field, and broad-brimmed black slouch hats were preferred to the regulation French-style képi. These hats were normally dressed with double gold cords terminating in two 'acorns'; the regulation badge was a black oval narrowly edged with gold, bearing an open-topped gold oakleaf wreath surrounding 'U.S.' in silver Old English lettering. Personal choice also affected other details of field attire, such as swords. Observers quickly noticed one visible difference between Western and Eastern armies: the latter followed uniform regulations closely, while Western soldiers exercised greater freedom of choice, and generally looked a rough-and-tumble bunch of men. When XI and XII Corps were transferred from the Army of the Potomac to the West in 1863 they were jeered by Western troops as 'band box soldiers.' Their generals reflected this attitude in more informal dress than was worn by Eastern generals.

A1: Brigadier-General Samuel Curtis
A2: Major-General John Frémont
A3: Major-General John McClernand

Samuel Curtis (A1), although graduated from West Point in 1831, spent little time in the army, and was unable to gain a regular commission again after commanding a regiment of Ohio volunteers in the Mexican War. As a brigadier-general of volunteers he was portrayed in full dress uniform, complete with the French-inspired feather-plumed *chapeaux-bras*, and massive gold bullion epaulettes bearing the single silver star of his rank. Note the black bow tie worn exposed at the front of the coat collar. His sword belt, with its circular clasp and chain link hangers, is non-regulation. Curtis was described as grave and undemonstrative in manner; nevertheless, he was noted for having a sentimental side, sometimes wandering by himself for hours looking for wildflowers. His long letters home describe exotic places and people he had seen in his travels.

The political appointee Nathaniel P.Banks may not have been much of a soldier, but he gloried in the uniform of his rank; here he poses in full dress, including the epaulettes rarely seen worn by many infinitely better commanders. *(Military Images)*

John Frémont (A2) was known as "The Pathfinder," and gloried in the fame which he had acquired during his explorations of the Western plains. He first appeared at his Missouri command dressed as he had during the Mexican War in California, in a civilian Western outfit including a light grey broad-brimmed hat, a brown coat with a flowing collar of paler color, and fringed leather leggings.

John McClernand (A3) was photographed in much less flamboyant regulation costume, although he, like Frémont, was a vain and self-important politician rather than a soldier. He wears a tall hat without a badge, and a plain frock coat without the regulation facings at collar and cuff. Like Frémont he is shown wearing the standard field belt and staff sword, without a buff sash.

B1: Major-General Nathaniel Banks
B2: Lieutenant-General Ulysses S.Grant
B3: Major-General Henry Halleck
Another Democratic Party politician given responsibilities far beyond his negligible military talents, Banks **(B1)** is shown posing in the uniform in which he often had himself photographed so that the voters back home could all see him as a bold warrior. Unlike most generals he wore the full dress sword belt and sash, and when in the field this stripped-down dress hat. Again, a broad black bow tie is worn outside the coat collar.

The image of Grant **(B2)** is taken partly from an accompanying photograph made shortly before the end of the war, in which he wears his short campaign coat open over a partly buttoned vest, and does not appear to wear a necktie. His binoculars are among the effects now preserved in the Civil War Library and Museum, Philadelphia.

When the Army of the Potomac reached the lines around Petersburg, Grant replaced his frock coat. According to Horace Porter, "The weather had become so warm that the general and most of the staff had ordered thin, dark-blue flannel blouses to be sent to them to take the place of the heavy uniform coats which they had been wearing.... The general's blouse, like the others was of plain material, single-breasted, and had four regulation brass buttons in front. It was substantially the coat of a private soldier, with nothing to indicate the rank of an officer except the three gold [silver] stars of a lieutenant-general on the shoulder-straps. He wore at this time a turn-down white linen collar and small black 'butterfly' cravat which was hooked on to his front collar-button."

U.S.Grant – fourth from right – and his staff, photographed towards the end of the war; see Plate B2. *(Military Images)*

Sylvanus Cadwallader noted: "When standing his ordinary attitude was that of having his head and shoulders thrown forward till he had the appearance of being a trifle round-shouldered. He also had an inveterate habit of thrusting both hands into the pockets of his pants when walking about headquarters or camp, and usually had a cigar clenched between his teeth, whether smoking, or not. It will be seen that he was no military 'dude.'"

Although there were attempts to promote Halleck **(B3)** in the popular press as a bold battlefield leader, in fact this fussy, pedantic engineer looked more like the "book soldier" he actually was. *Harper's Weekly* for 9 August 1862 commented that he looked like "some oleaginous Methodist parson dressed in regimentals, with a wide, stiff-rimmed black felt hat sticking on the back of his head, at an acute angle to the ground..."

C1: Major-General William Rosecrans
C2: Major-General Don Carlos Buell
C3: Major-General Edward Canby
Three generals who held independent Western commands, and showed some similarities of character as well as differences.

Rosecrans **(C1)**, by background an engineer – like so many of West Point's leading talents – had impressive intellectual gifts that were not often demonstrated by decisive performance in the field; he did not distinguish himself at Chickamauga and Chattanooga, and thereafter was given no serious employment. A devout student of the Roman Catholic faith, he often held long discussions about religion with staff members and other interested parties. Nevertheless, in portraits he has a smiling and open expression, and witnesses testified to his easy and pleasant manner with the common soldiers. Newspaperman Whitlaw Reid described Rosecrans as "nearly six feet high, compact,

with little waste flesh, nervous and active in all his movements, from the dictation of a dispatch to the tearing and chewing of his inseparable companion, the cigar."

Buell (C2), who was replaced by Rosecrans at the head of the Army of the Ohio in October 1862, was also relieved of his command for being too conservative a fighter. Unlike the equally bookish Rosecrans, however, this gifted administrator was known for his reserved manner, and was a stern disciplinarian.

Although Canby (C3) had a poor record at West Point and was initially sent to the frontier as a young infantry officer, he won good opinons in the Mexican War and blossomed as a talented staff officer, well known for his deep study of military law. Here he carries a leather map case slung from his shoulder to hip, but it is as likely to contain a copy of Army Regulations as maps. A portrait – see page 10 – shows rather

"turtle-like" lines around the mouth and chin, large protruding ears, and eyes and a mouth capable of good humour.

D1: Major-General Edward Ord
D2: Major-General James McPherson
D3: Major-General Jefferson C.Davis
Ord **(D1)** was one of those soldiers who served well but never attracted much attention in the press, or seems to have made a strong impression on his contemporaries. A competent divisional and corps commander, he was twice wounded in action during the war. A portrait shows strong, rather heavy features, a jutting nose, greying brown hair, and a darker mustache growing into large sidewhiskers.

By contrast, the other two figures on this plate drew a great deal of attention, if for very different reasons. McPherson **(D2)** – whose death in action in July 1864

Sherman – Plate E2 – dictates a message in the field in this sketch from *Harper's Weekly*.

OPPOSITE **Jefferson C.Davis, left – see Plate D3 – in his field headquarters tent with an aide, either a major or lieutenant-colonel. Note the paperwork crammed into the campaign desk. (*Military Images*)**

prompted a sorrowing Sherman to write that he could have become general-in-chief of the armies – combined a brilliant mind with an attractive personality, which earned him the respect and trust of his superiors and the affection of his equals and subordinates.

Here he holds a small compass while examining siege works at Vicksburg; many generals, and all engineers (like McPherson), carried such compasses, which came in a variety of styles. Some had a small, flip-up pointer so the compass could also be used as a sundial to check one's pocket watch. His uniform is regulation apart from the shallow-crowned slouch hat.

Jefferson C.Davis (D3) – who must have regretted his name many times during the war, especially as he was suspected by some of Southern sympathies – wears completely regulation clothing, with the addition of this black and gold sword belt, and his binoculars. He shaved his upper cheeks but wore a heavy mustache and beard. We have illustrated him holding an M1860 Colt 0.44in. Army pattern revolver, one of which he had borrowed on 29 September 1862 to shoot his commanding officer, Maj.Gen. Nelson, in a hotel lobby in Louisville, Kentucky. The Colt Army was a favorite of mounted troops, while foot officers preferred the lighter M1851 0.36in. Colt Navy revolver.

E1: Major-General Oliver Howard
E2: Major-General William T.Sherman
E3: Major-General Henry Slocum

The devout O.O.Howard (E1) wears regulation general's uniform, but a portrait shows the empty right sleeve pinned up as shown here. Note how he also wears his coat buttoned to the left, with the lapels buttoned back, exposing a blue vest with brass buttons, cut high at the neck over a stiff-collared white shirt and black bow tie. Many generals preferred to button the lapels back like this rather than wear the coat buttoned across all the way up to the collar.

One private in Sherman's (E2) army, Robert Strong from Illinois, saw the general as he inspected the front lines: "He had on an old slouch hat, pulled well down over his face to keep the rain off; wore a rubber blanket, high boots with spurs; and had a sword hanging at his side." The "gum blanket" illustrated is the standard Union soldier's issue; Sherman's slouch hat is preserved in the Smithsonian Institution. John Pope recalled his "lofty beak and bristling mustache... pleasant smile and kindly manner..."

Frank Haskell described Slocum (E3) at Gettysburg: "Slocum is small, rather spare, with black, straight hair and beard, which latter is unshaven and thin, large, full, quick, black eyes, white skin, sharp nose, wide cheek bones, and hollow cheeks and small chin. His movements are quick and angular, and he dresses with a sufficient degree of elegance."

One portrait photograph shows a spade-pointed beard low on the jawline leaving the upper part of the chin shaved. Here he wears the regulation dark blue képi, but decorated with black quarter-braiding.

F1: Major-General Peter Osterhaus
F2: Major-General John Schofield
F3: Major-General George H.Thomas

The German-born and -trained Osterhaus (F1) kneels to retrieve something from one of the trunks that – as a general officer – he was allowed to carry with him in the field. Sherman disliked his officers, even up to general rank, travelling with much camp equipage – something that he

complained George Thomas too often allowed. Still, generals did need to carry much beyond personal items, in the way of forms, maps, reports, and books. Most also carried mess kits containing plates, drinking vessels, and cutlery, often made of tinned iron. Osterhaus had reddish auburn hair, light blue eyes, and a pale complexion much marked by freckles. He wears regulation uniform, with a plain, unbraided képi.

Schofield **(F2)** was photographed with his sandy beard falling to the fifth coat button. He sits on the most common type of camp chair used by Union Army officers, a folding design which compressed fairly flat for stowing in head-quarters wagons. (Some Union enlisted men reported that they never sat on a chair during the entire war, and it took the better part of years to get used to them again when they returned to civilian life).

Brigadier-General John Beatty noted that Thomas **(F3)** "is tall, heavy, sedate; whiskers and head grayish. Puts on less style... and is a modest, gentlemanly, reliable soldier." Despite his rather forbidding expression "Old Pap" was very popular with his men, who presumably recognized that his always deliberate preparations for battle saved lives. Here – against the background of a house used as the headquarters of his Army of the Cumberland – he examines a map carried in a black leather mapcase that is designed to roll up to protect the contents from weather. The Union Army was able to print multiple copies of the same map from plates that it could make in the field and print on traveling presses. This was a great advantage; all officers in any command could be confident that they were working from the same information.

G1: Brigadier-General James Wilson
G2: Colonel Benjamin Grierson
G3: Brigadier-General Judson Kilpatrick
These three figures depict the best-known cavalry com-manders of the Western theater. Note that all three carry the French-inspired M1860 light cavalry saber.

Wilson **(G1)** was photographed in a uniform which from any distance would have been indistinguishable from that of one of his troopers: a képi with a black band and the general officers' badge; a plain dark blue short jacket – much as worn by many enlisted cavalrymen – with 12 small front buttons and three at the cuff, with his single silver star sewn directly to the shoulders; and enlisted men's sky-blue trousers with no stripes down the legs. This shows the evolution from a special dress for generals and other senior officers early in the war, to one that mimicked that worn by the fighting men – a deliberate attempt to prevent enemy sharpshooters from picking out these valuable targets. The young general is examining the Spencer repeating carbine which he managed to secure for his troops.

Grierson **(G2)** is shown here in the uniform of a colonel of cavalry, in which he won his fame leading a raid into Mississippi. The frock coat has two rows of nine buttons set evenly, and gold-edged shoulder straps in cavalry yellow bearing the silver eagle of his rank; the sky-blue trousers also have yellow trim. The plume in his slouch hat is probably taken from his regulation dress hat.

Kilpatrick **(G3)** wore a variety of uniforms, most of which were only slightly regulation. He was noted as wearing a slouch hat as well as the képi shown here, with its black quarter-braiding and silver star. Here, like Wilson, he displays

OPPOSITE **Hugh Judson Kilpatrick – Plate G3 – in an** early war and entirely non-regulation uniform, before becoming a general. *(Military Images)*

RIGHT **Francis Blair Jr – Plate H3 – as pictured in** *Harper's Weekly* **on 17 August 1861,** when he was still in colonel's uniform and had yet to grow his full beard.

his rank star sewn directly to his shoulders; on his other uniforms he wore shoulder straps, but they differed from the regulation style in having only a very narrow gold edge. He also liked to affect a tie stick-pin that featured a gilt prancing horse.

H1: Major-General Alpheus Williams
H2: Major-General John Logan
H3: Major-General Francis Blair

Depicted here with his trusty flask, Williams **(H1)** was known to take a drink or two from time to time. While there was a temperance movement in the country it was not yet strong, and heavy drinking was more a norm among all classes than something out of the ordinary.

Just before the war began the Army adopted a new staff and staff corps sword – a light, straight-bladed weapon with few good fighting qualities. By adopting this design the Army admitted that generals and their staff officers were not expected to see much hand-to-hand combat. Few generals or their staffs wore this sword during the war; the fiery "Black Jack" Logan **(H2)** is shown here examining one rather dubiously. George W.Nichols wrote that no one who met Logan was likely to forget his striking appearance.

We depict Logan's less passionate but equally effective rival Blair **(H3)** as he checks his pocket watch. At this period there were no standard time zones, which would come later under pressure from railroads, and times were quite different from city to city, let alone from state to state. The times of events at Gettysburg, for example, recorded by the two opposing armies, were about a half hour different. This made co-ordination difficult, and everyone responsible for operations had to check constantly with both the army's time (officially kept within each regiment by its sergeant-major) and local times.

INDEX